DURHAM

Text by
DOUGLAS POCOC[K]

Photographs by
ERNEST FRANKL

PEVENSEY
Heritage Guides

Durham

A lofty sandy outcrop encircled by a loop of the meandering River Wear, is surmounted by the imperious piles of Durham Cathedral and castle rising above the old city. Little traffic is allowed to rumble along the outcrop's steep and winding streets, leaving the stroller in peace to explore the tree-shrouded pathways that shelve away to the river, or the wide, spacious greens on the plateau top. The monks of Lindisfarne, fleeing from the Vikings and taking with them the body of the revered 7th-century bishop and hermit St Cuthbert, found sanctuary on the outcrop in 995. From these humble beginnings arose the might of Durham's Prince-Bishops, whom the kings of England allowed to rule, from their twin strongholds of cathedral and castle, as uncrowned monarchs of the north-east, to keep the marauding Scots at bay.

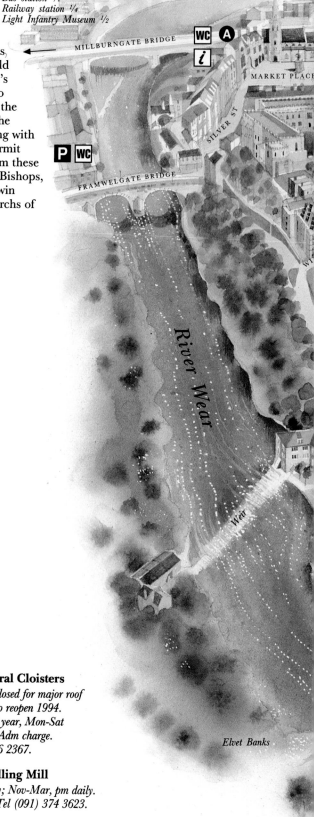

A 690
Bus station ¼
Railway station ¼
Light Infantry Museum ½

MILLBURNGATE BRIDGE

MARKET PLACE

SILVER ST

FRAMWELGATE BRIDGE

River Wear

Weir

Elvet Banks

PLACES TO SEE

Ⓐ Town Hall and Guildhall
At one corner of the Market Place, the Church of St Nicholas raises its tall spire above the Town Hall, a simple Victorian building with chapel-like windows. Adjoining the Town Hall is the more elaborate Guildhall, with large traceried windows and a spired turret on its roof.
Town Hall and Guildhall: All year, Mon-Fri. Free entry. Tel (091) 386 6111.

Ⓑ Durham Castle
Clinging to the cliffs above the River Wear, its flanks bristling with battlements and huge retaining buttresses, it is little wonder that Durham Castle was the only northern fortress never to fall to the Scots. Inside the courtyard, where parapets rise towards the octagonal keep high on its mound, the strong lines of the fortress have been softened a little by the castle's subsequent history as Bishop's Palace, and then as University College.
Tours: First three weeks Apr, and July-Sept, daily; other months, pm Mon, Wed and Sat. Adm charge. Tel (091) 386 5481.

Ⓒ Durham Cathedral
Palace Green is dwarfed by Durham Cathedral's two great western towers, four-spired east end, and a central tower whose 218ft height is almost matched by the length of the nave. So huge is the cathedral that it almost runs out of room, for the west end teeters above the River Wear, making it necessary to enter the building through the north door.

Ⓓ Cathedral Cloisters
Dormitory: Closed for major roof repairs; due to reopen 1994. Treasury: All year, Mon-Sat and pm Sun. Adm charge. Tel (091) 386 2367.

Ⓔ Old Fulling Mill
Apr-Oct, daily; Nov-Mar, pm daily. Adm charge. Tel (091) 374 3623.

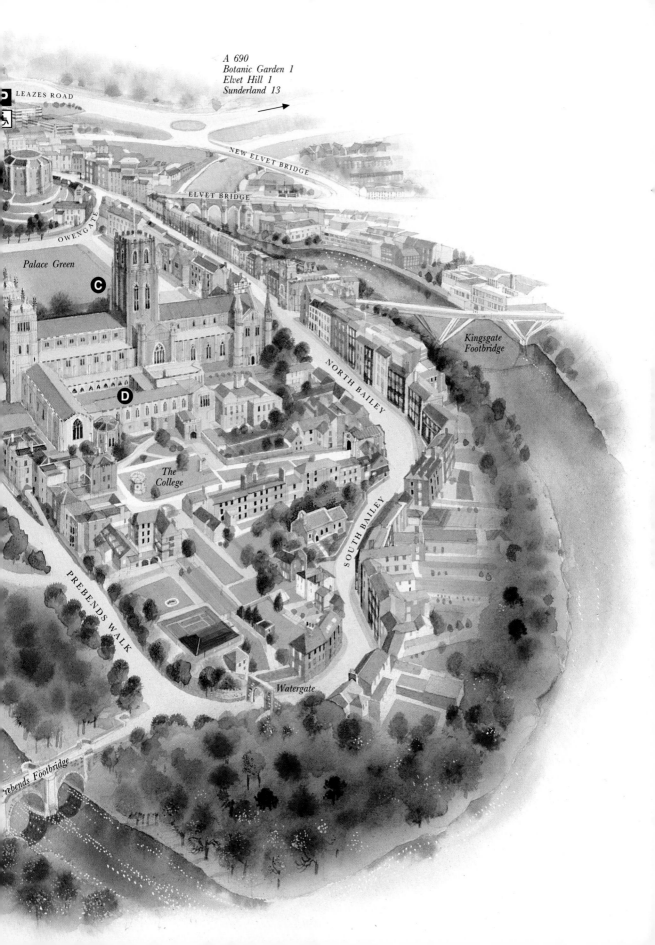

A Pevensey Heritage Guide

Copyright © 1993 Ernest Frankl, Douglas Pocock, The Pevensey Press

First published 1993

Photographs: Ernest Frankl

Colour map copyright © The Reader's Digest Association Ltd

A catalogue record for this book is available from the British Library.

ISBN 0 907115 66 7

Design by Book Production Consultants, Cambridge
Printed in Hong Kong by Wing King Tong Co. Ltd
for David & Charles plc
Brunel House Newton Abbot Devon

The Pevensey Press is an imprint of David & Charles plc

Front cover
The classic view of Durham, with the towers of the Cathedral and the wooded banks of the gorge of the River Wear.

Back cover
No. 16, The College seen through the archway of the Gatehouse, looking from the South Bailey into The College (the Cathedral Close); The Romanesque-style Galilee Chapel, at the west end of the Cathedral; the monogram of Christ and the crossed keys of St Peter's Monkwearmouth (Sunderland). The church is on the site of the monastery founded by Benedict Biscop in 674.

Title page inset
Durham Cathedral was built to contain the shrine of St Cuthbert. This modern wooden carving by Fenwick Lawson in the Cathedral Cloister depicts the saint as the Lindisfarne contemplative.

Contents

1 Introduction

Durham is a city which medieval writers likened to Jerusalem, which Ruskin termed one of the wonders of the world and which Pevsner, more modestly, called one of the architectural experiences of Europe. Experience is heightened by anticipation, which, for the alert traveller, may be prompted by a glimpse of the central tower of the Cathedral when still many miles distant. Nearer the city all views are hidden until the last moment when, as the visitor arrives on the edge of the bowl within which the city is set, Cathedral and Castle rise with theatrical drama. There has been no gradual build-up of suburbia: the change from countryside to city is almost as abrupt as in the medieval world when a city wall sharply divided the two realms. The rail traveller from the south and the motorist via the A1(M) arriving at the Bede roundabout both encounter this unforgettable delayed and sudden revelation.

The centre of the bowl is occupied by what is known locally as the Peninsula, an upstanding river-girt area from which the name of Durham is derived – Dunholm, 'hill-island'. The Cathedral and Castle rise from this hill-island to provide the architectural climax and distinctive silhouette which have inspired eulogies in verse and on canvas, in scholarship and in international travel guides. More recently the two buildings have been designated a World Heritage Site.

The sharpness of profile is emphasised by the green collar of the wooded river banks. The incision is very recent in geological terms, dating from the end of the last Ice Age, as do the sands and gravels which form the undulating rim of the basin. To those with the eye of faith the undulations are seven in number, as befits a holy city. They certainly provide a series of eminences from which to observe the city. The River Wear meanders through the basin on its northward journey. The reason for the river's backward loop within the basin to form the hill-island is a mystery, since it is cut into solid rock, but its subsequent advantage for building foundation is obvious. The depth of the gorge and the softness of the present foliage both emphasise and complement the height and strength embodied in the castellated stonework of Cathedral and Castle. The river and its valley also represent the invasion of the countryside into the heart of the city. That this is no ornamental, manicured urban park is shown by the green skylines visible from almost any part of the city centre and the panorama from the top of the Cathedral tower confirms that the green rim is no trick of intervisibility.

The memorable architectural climax dominates the rest of the urban scene, where height, mass and siting all defer to provide a foil, an architecture of human scale, which leads the eye upwards to the monument on the hill. Within the town the general urban layout or texture is one of complexity without confusion, and it has an air of mystery. The lattice of streets is not immediately legible, having a geometry in harmony with the undulating relief. Durham knows the secret of suggestion and avoids the boredom which

1 The visitor to Durham is immediately struck by the city's wealth of ornate doorways. This is the entrance to Bishop Cosin's Hall, Palace Green. Remodelled in the 18th century as the Archdeacon's Inn, the building became a University hall in 1857 when it acquired its present name. It is now part of University College.

7

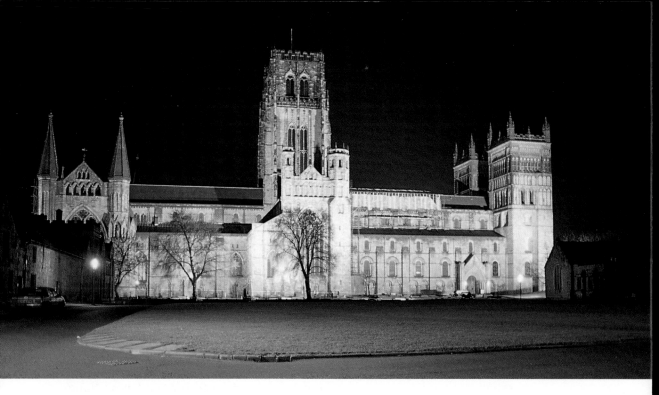

comes from revelation without effort. A succession of curves and corners and of enclosed or restricted vistas encourages the visitor to explore, to convert mystery into surprise, and surprise into an increasingly rich and rewarding tapestry. Throughout this exploration the silhouette of Castle and Cathedral provides orientation.

2 The floodlit north face of the Cathedral, seen across Palace Green from the head of Owengate. Four centuries of medieval architecture here blend into a dramatic unity.

The organic geometry of the streets is filled out with an urban design where the vernacular of largely anonymous architects blends to create a unity in diversity. Each street, whether narrow (Silver Street, **Saddler Street** (**5**), the Baileys, for instance), or open (Old Elvet, South Street) shows a rhythm in its variety. Open spaces may be lined in similar harmony – the Market Place, Palace Green, The College. Even the backs of buildings, exposed by the city's rolling topography, exhibit good-neighbourliness among themselves – the gaggle of buildings of Back Silver Street, seen from across the river, is a perfect example.

The attraction of Durham's townscape has its origin in our ancestors' listening to what the landscape had to say and building responsively. The Normans positioned the **Cathedral** (**2,3**) centrally, astride the hard-rock Peninsula, and the Castle at the northern end, at the same time allowing an intimate street pattern to evolve in the town below. The surrounding greenery is also a Norman legacy handed down to later ecclesiastical authorities, for whom aesthetics and conservation slowly came to the fore. In the 1830s, when the newly founded University inherited several of the Church's buildings on the Peninsula, including the Castle, it also inherited its care for the environment. In the second half of the 20th century, the University has added considerably to the city's architectural richness, with ten of its buildings receiving national awards or commendations. The importance contemporary planning authorities attach to sight-lines, particularly with regard to the Peninsula and to the rim of the basin, represents their technical response to the sense of place adhering to this historic city. The result is a rich heritage to explore.

2 History

The story of Durham begins in the 7th century with Cuthbert, a shepherd boy in the Borders called to the religious life in the community founded by Aidan on Lindisfarne (Holy Island) off the Northumberland coast. He was subsequently elected Bishop and canonised after his death in 687. Many miracles were associated with his name; moreover, after his death his body was said to have suffered no physical deterioration. It was doubly natural therefore that the community should take the body of their saint with them when they evacuated their exposed island in the face of Viking raids in the 9th century. For over a hundred years the community – now known as the Cuthbert Community – was re-established in Chester-le-Street, 6 miles north of Durham. Then, threatened with further Viking raids, they once more became peripatetic, wandering as far south as Ripon before returning north again. They were probably on their way back to Chester-le-Street when the defensive qualities of Durham attracted them. Legend, recounted in Scott's poem 'Marmion', tells of the saint's intervening to select his final resting place, a maid and her dun cow taking a decisive role in confirming its siting. (The carving of milkmaids and cow on the Cathedral exterior is a later generation's transfer of legend to stone.) What is certain is that the community, complete with Cuthbert's coffin and treasures, and with extensive privileges, found a permanent home in Durham in 995.

A stone cathedral worthy to contain the shrine of St Cuthbert was completed in 1017 and became the greatest centre of pilgrimage in the country. Among the early pilgrims was King Canute, who granted further tracts of land and privileges to the community. The attraction was further enhanced by the addition of the remains of the Venerable Bede in 1022, brought from the nearby monastery at Jarrow by Aelfred the Sacrist.

The hill-island Peninsula thus became the focus of subsequent growth rather than other local sites which had been occupied earlier. On a river terrace under the brow of the Peninsula, for instance, was the earlier Saxon settlement of Aelfet ee (Swan Island), the present Elvet. To the south, half a mile up-river, the same terrace has yielded evidence of a Roman villa at what is today known as Old Durham (Maiden Castle), sited on part of the perimeter rim, here sharpened by river action.

The site chosen by, or for, St Cuthbert was mightily confirmed by the conquering Normans. In a strategic buffer zone on the east coast lowland route to Scotland, the recent Saxon fortifications on a naturally defensible peninsula had already been proved in withstanding two attacks from Scottish armies in 1006 and 1038. The first description of the city, dating from the early 12th century, emphasised its situation: 'This city is renowned throughout all Britain, set on steep slopes and marvellously built with rocks all round. A strongly running river flows past enclosed by weirs.' (The description, probably composed in the monastery at Durham, is significant in

its own right, since it constitutes this country's last extant Old English or Anglo-Saxon poem.)

William the Conqueror therefore chose Durham, rather than Newcastle (his new castle) on the Tyne 14 miles north, as the centre of Norman administration in northern England and as a bulwark against the Scots. To oversee the extensive area stretching to the Scottish border the King instituted a line of non-hereditary prince-bishops, the first of whom was Walcher of Lorraine (1071–80). Rulers in both spiritual and temporal matters, they enjoyed full royal rights and privileges within the prince-bishopric or palatinate, possessing their own mint, exchequer, parliament, judiciary and army. The various offices were located around what is known as **Palace Green** (**4**), the Palace or Castle being the residence of the Prince-Bishop.

The city itself proclaimed visually the authority and power of the new rulers of England; the evidence of Saxon beginnings was erased. A new castle was begun on the site of the old one in 1072 at the vulnerable northern neck of the Peninsula, the only side not protected by the encircling river. By the early 12th century a strong stone wall replaced wooden ramparts around the whole of the Peninsula. The Saxon cathedral, which had taken 20 years to construct, was demolished and replaced by a 40-year Anglo-Norman project begun in 1093 under Bishop William of St Carileph (or St Calais) (1081–96). This new Cathedral, even more than the Castle, was a show of imperial force, its size – and, internally, its massive pillars in particular – suggesting it was indeed, in Sir Walter Scott's phrase, 'half castle 'gainst the Scot'. Associated with the Cathedral, a new abbey arose for a Benedictine monastic order which replaced the existing, more loosely organised community. The area between the Cathedral and the Castle was cleared of housing, on grounds of pollution

3 The south face of the Cathedral with buildings of The College just visible through the trees. One hundred feet below the Cathedral is the encircling river; beyond is the green skyline which characteristically bounds the city.

10

and fire hazard; the inhabitants were probably resettled at Framwellgate. Two bridges were placed either side of the neck of the Peninsula – Framwellgate (1128) to the small community on the west bank, and Elvet (1160) to the ancient borough of that name. Northwards, a hospital and the Church of St Giles completed the major components of Norman Durham. Collectively they have provided an indelible imprint.

By late medieval times the general form had consolidated rather than changed. The earliest existing maps of Durham, by Matthew Patteson in 1595 and John Speed in 1610, show the formerly extramural Market Place now incorporated within the city's walls, with major roads winding their way from the two bridges and along the Claypath spine. This general form was quaintly likened by the author Robert Hegge (1599–1629) to a crab, 'supposing the city for its belly and the suburbs for its claws'. The linear development linked the core with the early communities at Elvet, Framwellgate/Crossgate and Gilesgate.

The fine detail in the perspective views of the early maps permits the earliest glimpse of many features in the major buildings and defences of the city – gates in the city wall, fortified towers on the peninsular side of the two bridges in the extended circuit of the wall, and weirs placed across the river to deepen the water and provide power for the mills.

During the intervening four centuries Durham had risen to its zenith in political and ecclesiastical prominence, a growth punctuated by skirmishes with the Scots, the 'auld enemy', by periodic famine, and by the shock waves of the Reformation. A measure of its importance as a medieval centre is the

4 *Looking north from the central tower of the Cathedral. Beyond Palace Green and the Castle keep, the spire of St Nicholas' Church pinpoints the Market Place. The encircling river lies to left and right.*

5 *Behind No. 50 Saddler Street is the bastion, a relict of the medieval defences. It formerly connected the keep (just visible at top) to Great Northgate, which spanned Saddler Street.*

6 *The University's Music School (1541), in a sylvan corner of Palace Green. For three centuries the building housed the Grammar School, until its transfer to a new site off the peninsula in 1844.*

number of visits to the city by royalty, mostly English, but also, during peaceful interludes, Scottish. The prince-bishops, in return for their privileges, had to maintain a fortified garrison and fighting unit. The forces saw frequent action, both locally and further north. In 1346, for instance, while Edward III was abroad, Bishop Neville helped to defeat the Scottish army in the western suburb now known as Neville's Cross. At Flodden Field (1513) historians have the odd problem of whether to ascribe victory to the contribution of the Bishop's army or to St Cuthbert's banner specially carried for the campaign.

The reputation and splendour of the Cathedral of St Cuthbert and its associated Abbey made the city an ecclesiastical focus of England. The transfer of the endowments of Jarrow and Monkwearmouth, gifts from early Norman bishops, and the general Benedictine emphasis on education and learning ensured that it was the intellectual centre of the North. Its manuscripts included the Lindisfarne Gospels, the earliest surviving great masterpiece of English medieval book painting, dating from the late 7th to early 8th century; its foundations included Durham College (later Trinity College), Oxford, where brothers were sent to complete their studies. Scholars, however, were far outnumbered by pilgrims flocking to a cathedral which contained not only the elaborate shrines to St Cuthbert and St Bede, and the head of a third northern saint, Oswald, but also a supporting assortment of holy relics ranging from a rib of the Virgin Mary and a piece of the manger to griffins' eggs. The elaborate shrine of the North's most famous saint was given a new setting in the 13th century, when advantage was taken of foundational problems to replace the simple apsidal east end of the Cathedral with a more impressive construction.

The splendour of ecclesiastic Durham, as well as the supremacy of Church over city, was eroded during the 16th and 17th centuries. The Reformation brought change but also continuity. The Cathedral was stripped of its shrines, relics and other embellishments – and also of its dedication to St Cuthbert – but not of its Bishop. The abbey was dissolved by Henry VIII but, happily, the transition was smooth; the Prior was successfully transformed into a

Dean, and 12 monks became Cathedral prebendaries or canons. If anything the changes had a greater impact on the city, which, always subservient to the Bishop, lost much of the trade connected with pilgrims, festivals and fairs. The growth of shops, lodging-houses and markets had been recognised as early as 1179 when Bishop le Puiset (1153–95) granted the first civic charter, but it was not until after the Reformation that the inhabitants were granted any degree of self-government and over a century later, after the Restoration, that they acquired parliamentary representation. During the Commonwealth and Protectorate the bishopric was temporarily abolished and the Dean and Chapter suppressed. Restoration of both came with Charles II, although the former balance of Church and city was never to be restored. Both, however, were slowly to enter upon a century of prosperity, which was reflected increasingly in elegant architecture and landscape. 'I must say of the whole Citty of Durham its the noblest, cleane and pleasant buildings, streets large well pirched,' commented Celia Fiennes on her visit in 1698.

Through time, Georgian structures – more often reconstructions – came to grace **The College** (**7,8**) and the Baileys on the Peninsula and in Old Elvet and South Street. The residences in the College, the former Abbey site, housed the so-called golden canons, renowned for being among the richest in the country. (Defoe had recorded the clergy living 'in all the magnificence and splendour imaginable'.) Along **the Baileys** (9), on the site of premises originally occupied by the Bishop's military tenants or barons, there were new town houses for county families, 'people of the first fortune' as Hutchinson called them. Their gardens extended to the old city wall and then formed hanging gardens down to the river. Life was certainly gracious for those at the top, and Durham, still over a week's journey from London, was now a sophisticated county town and cultural centre. In the season the citizen might attend horse racing, go to the theatre in Saddler Street, dance or play cards in the Assembly Rooms, entertain – or just promenade.

Promenading became increasingly fashionable with the emergence of the English taste for the picturesque, for 'composed' landscape. From this period stemmed the active landscape gardening of the river banks by the Dean and Chapter. Previously the slopes below the Cathedral and Castle in particular had been bare – and known as Bishop's Waste – but now an active programme of planting and path-making sought to produce amid the teasing topography a series of contrived vistas that is still one of Durham's greatest delights. In 1752 the poet Thomas Gray was one of the first to record his pleasure:

> I have one of the most beautiful Vales in England to walk in with prospects that change every ten steps, and open up something new wherever I turn me, all rude and romantic, in short the sweetest Spot to break your neck or drown yourself in that ever was beheld.

A visual climax was provided in 1778 when Prebends' Bridge, named for the prebendaries who financed it, replaced an earlier and more modest construction destroyed by floods.

Notable as a county town, Durham developed little manufacturing industry, although it did claim the first production of mustard in the world in 1720. There is no reason to suppose that more would have arisen had any of the four 18th-century schemes to make the Wear navigable from Durham to

9 *Modest 17th- and 18th-century town houses in the North Bailey. Most are now owned by the University; no. 38, shown here, is the home of the Classics Department.*

its mouth and to the Tyne come to pass (the statue of Neptune in the Market Place is a reminder of the intentions), for a new form of locomotion was about to appear which, in association with the rapidly increasing exploitation of coal, was to change the face of the region.

Although 19th-century county Durham possessed the country's most productive coalfield and saw the birth of rail transport, the county town itself remained largely unaffected by the industrial expansion of the age. The coal seams under the centre of the city were generally too thin for large-scale economic exploitation, while lack of early interest among rail entrepreneurs as much as opposition accounted for the late and circuitous connection to the rail network. The lack of suitable level sites and water transport put Durham at a disadvantage compared with many other centres. Population figures summarise the consequent shift in fortune: in 1801, with a population of 7,500, it had only recently conceded first place in the county to Sunderland; by the end of the century the county figure had increased tenfold and the county town, with a population of 16,000, had slipped to 12th position. Industrial urban growth along the river estuaries of the Tyne and Tees across the county boundary gave it even lower ranking regionally.

The unenthusiastic response to industrial development meant that Durham did not undergo the marked character change typical of so many English towns. A dozen or so streets of bye-law housing to the west of the Peninsula – they provide the foreground of the rail passenger's vista of the Cathedral –

suggest what might have been, but topography, if not land-ownership, prevented any emergence of a Victorian collar to the central core. Durham's manufacturing was characteristically that of a small county town serving itself and a restricted hinterland, destined for eclipse as technological advance favoured specialised centres. Its chief activities were corn and paper milling, brewing and malting, iron and brass founding, worsted spinning and wool combing. But two initiatives have grown to serve worldwide markets: organ construction and carpet-making. Mackay's quality carpets, which floor many an international hotel and ocean liner, can trace their lineage through earlier woollen and linen industries. The organs of Harrison and Harrison, which have been installed in nearly half the cathedrals of the country as well as in major churches and civic buildings around the world, began as a Rochdale business but soon moved to Durham in 1872 on the encouragement of John Bacchus Dykes, Canon of the Cathedral and the most prolific Victorian composer of hymn tunes.

Rather than become an industrial centre, Durham found it more natural to foster the creation of England's third university. Given its tradition of learning, and the distance to the academic centres at Oxford and Cambridge, the possibility of a university in the North had been twice previously considered – at the Reformation and during the Commonwealth, times when the assets of the Church might be diverted to such a project. Henry VIII's consideration was brief, but Oliver Cromwell, following a petition, issued letters patent in 1657 for a college with provost, scholars and exhibitioners. The first fellows were appointed but almost immediately Cromwell died, the monarchy was restored and the revenues reverted to the reconstituted Dean and Chapter. Political reform and its possible effect on ecclesiastical revenue were to the fore again in 1832, when Bishop van Mildert (1826–36) piloted a Durham University Bill through Parliament. The initiative was jointly that of the Dean and Chapter and the Bishop; both provided income and accommodation, the latter including several buildings on Palace Green, not least, in 1837, the Bishop's Palace – the Castle. Their action deflected the possible confiscation of revenues from the see of Durham in the imminent Reform Bill. They were also spurred by the rumours of a possible university in London and in other provincial cities. From the point of view of townscape, the decision of 1832 was a stabilising influence ensuring respect for the existing buildings given to the new foundation and those subsequently acquired or commissioned.

10 *The early 19th-century Crown Courts (formerly Assize Courts) on the green in Old Elvet. They were designed and built in the classical Tuscan style by the leading Durham architect Ignatius Bonomi.*

11 *Looking upriver from Baths Bridge as two crews approach the finish in Durham's annual regatta. First held in 1834, the event is the country's oldest regatta, attracting racing clubs from all over the world.*

The Bishop's residence was transferred to its present location at Bishop Auckland; other establishments to leave the Peninsula for new locations about this time were the public school (to an extensive green site on Church land on the other side of Prebends' Bridge, 1844), the gaol, and **Assize Court (10)** (to Old Elvet after removal of the last and most impressive of the original city gates at the head of Saddler Street in 1820) and the County Hospital (to the western fringe of the city in 1860). The streets of the city also lost a more unsavoury medieval legacy; paving or, more commonly, cobbling was completed in the 1820s and 1830s, although it was at once disturbed by the laying of subterranean gas, water and, finally, sewer pipelines. The first facility, according to the then recently established city newspaper, enabled night-time illumination to replace 'notorious nocturnal darkness'.

The changing structures and powers of local government made other significant and permanent changes to the face of Durham during the 19th century. The Market Place was reshaped in the 1860s. The west side gained a new town hall and market building; the north side was lined by a rebuilt St Nicholas' Church; diagonally opposite, two banks contributed additional dignity. County links, of which the prominent equestrian statue of Lord Londonderry in the Market Place and the miners' headquarters in a new North Road provide contrasting symbols, were formalised by a large Shire Hall in Old Elvet. But the construction which perhaps best symbolises the century in Durham is the multi-arched and curving railway viaduct. Bridging one of the gullied re-entrants in the west of the surrounding rim, its lofty but peripheral position symbolises how 19th-century industrial power, so near, yet passed by the town. The viaduct was not built until 1857, and not until 1872 was direct connection of the present route made from London to Newcastle.

The Durham scene has seen much change in the 20th century. In terms of population growth, however, there was a long pause between the two World Wars: the inter-war decline in the county's basic industries and the era of general economic and social depression meant that the 1951 census figure of 19,000 was no higher than that for 1921. But that did not prevent the beginnings of several significant structural changes. Clearance of slum property near the waterside in Framwellgate, with resettlement of the displaced community on the plateau rim to the north-east at Gilesgate in the 1930s, was a centrifugal process observable also in the University, which began building south of the river in 1924, and in the Hospital's move to its extensive northern site from 1942. Along the western ridge a sequence of roads, in part quickly lined with ribbon development, was linked to form a new Great North Road through Neville's Cross, by-passing the centre of the city for the first time.

During the most recent era of growth the census population figures had reached 25,000 by 1974, when local government reorganisation redrew the map of the county, dividing it into 8 units, with the central one incorporating, and taking the name, City of Durham. Today there is a coherent urban entity containing nearly half of the new district's 80,000 population, but the essential quality of 'Durhamness' has been respected, so that present-day experience of arriving in the city and exploring it has scarcely been diluted. The most extensive residential growth, for instance, is beyond the rim of the central basin on estates to the east (Gilesgate Moor–Carrville–Belmont) and north (Framwellgate Moor–Newton Hall). Nearer, but still beyond the crest of the rim, the wooded northern slopes accommodate a new county hall, police headquarters, land registry, museum and hospital. Southwards, the gently rising land, also well wooded and undulating, has been carefully studded with University buildings – mainly half a dozen colleges and the science laboratories. The sensitivity of their placement within the landscape is confirmed both by the view from the Cathedral tower and on entering the city along South Road. Lastly, the city has withstood the worst ravages of motorised traffic – in fact, advantages have been extracted in response to its demands. The Great North Road has been moved from the western suburbs to the other side of the city, 2 miles distant, with motorway status. Admittedly an inner relief road of the 1960s, breaching the neck of the Peninsula (which the river failed to achieve), blasted a hole in the landscape but the Claypath building line is due for reinstatement, and a new entry vista was opened up. According to Ian Nairn, a strong critic of much new development, the created view was 'superb' and the project illustrated how 'a new road can improve a cathedral city'.

Durham's qualities have been recognised throughout history. In modern times the recognition has been official, resulting in protective legislation. In 1968, following the 1967 Civic Amenities Act, the city's central core was designated a Conservation Area: one of the few to be classified as having outstanding status. In 1980 the boundaries of the Conservation Area were extended outwards and more realistically redrawn in relation to the surrounding rim. The city is on the list of towns designated as significant by the Council of British Archaeology. In 1981, during the Campaign for Urban Renaissance, the Council of Europe selected Durham as one of its five demonstration sites in the United Kingdom. In 1987 came the ultimate accolade when the Castle and Cathedral were declared a World Heritage Site.

3 The Cathedral

The Cathedral or abbey-church of Durham, besides being the spiritual focus of city and diocese, is outstanding aesthetically, historically and architecturally.

Most obviously, the Cathedral is a very visible building, whether from afar or near at hand. It can be seen from surrounding hills and from the rim around the city, from the bridges and riverside within the city and close at hand on the Peninsula. Little wonder that it has been depicted in a whole series of paintings and sketches made from the numerous vantage points over the centuries. Perhaps three of these points in particular have been favoured above all – from Prebends' Bridge, South Street and Observatory Hill, as recorded in the paintings of Turner, Cotman and Carmichael respectively. Travellers and diarists have expressed in words their reaction to the same views. Matthew Arnold, in a letter referring to his travels in 1861, praised all three:

> When you cross the Wear by the Prebends' Bridge and, ascending through its beautiful skirt of wood, plant yourself on the hill opposite the cathedral, the view of the cathedral and castle together is superb; even Oxford has no view to compare with it ... I was most agreeably disappointed, for I had fancied Durham rising out of a cinder bed. I finished by the observatory, a point on a higher range than the hill just in face of the cathedral, but commanding much the same view in greater perspective.

12 The Norman nave of the Cathedral Church of Christ and the Blessed Virgin Mary, looking east. This extensive view of nave through to choir dates from the 1840s when Cosin's wooden screen, with organ above, was removed. The present, lighter marble screen was erected in the 1870s, the work of Sir Gilbert Scott. Scott was also responsible for removing the whitewash to expose the warm colour of the natural stone.

The prejudice of his southern expectations may cause a smile, but the scholarly and cosmopolitan Nikolaus Pevsner, in the Durham volume of his *The Buildings of England* series, is equally enthusiastic. Of all the prospects in Durham, he considered that from Prebends' Bridge the 'most moving', and he surely had the view from South Street in mind when he wrote 'Durham is one of the great experiences of Europe to the eyes of those who appreciate architecture, and to the minds of those who understand architecture. The group of Cathedral, Castle and Monastery on the rock can only be compared to Avignon and Prague.' The view from the railway induced Ruskin to call Durham one of the wonders of the world, and impressed J. B. Priestley, in his *English Journey*, with the 'Macbeth-like look of the city'.

The centrality of the Cathedral in these grand views of Durham has given them cultural and spiritual as well as architectural significance of which Sharp wrote eloquently:

Every cathedral city was designed to be a perpetual memorial to the history, continuity, struggles and, in part anyway, the triumph of the Christian Faith, on which European civilisation is largely founded. So heightened is this function at Durham by nature of the tremendous setting that the question of its mutilation becomes a matter of moment not merely to Durham or Britain but to Christendom.

Sharp, a nationally recognised town planning consultant, was writing under the wartime threat of a power station, to be sited a mile downstream from the Cathedral, which also drew a first leader in *The Times* arguing for retention of a scene where the visible imprint of the Norman Conquest was 'without parallel in England'.

In terms of architecture, the Cathedral is the greatest Romanesque (Norman) church in Europe. It is a building by which others are judged. It was the first cathedral in England to be designated a World Heritage Site by U.N.E.S.C.O. (1987). On the 150th anniversary of the Royal Institute of British Architects, three years earlier, it had been voted the best building in the world. (The voting was among 58 eminent people 'interested in the quality and standards of architecture' who were asked by the *Illustrated London News* to list the world's ten best buildings. For the record, the Taj Mahal was second and the Parthenon third.) The Romanesque building particularly impresses students of architecture in that it contains three major elements anticipating the Gothic era – flying buttresses, ribbed vaulting and pointed arches. It was at Durham that the thrust problem was resolved – one of the great discoveries of European civilisation – and a large building completely vaulted in stone.

With hindsight it is possible to say that the Cathedral church was destined to be an imposing one. Both general location and detailed site fitted the Normans' plan for the settlement of England and for a bulwark against the Scots. They therefore capitalised on the Saxon beginnings. A Norman line of bishops was introduced in 1071, Bishop Walcher being the first, and the loosely organised religious community of St Cuthbert was reformed and a celibate monastic order established (1083). Given the regal powers and privileges of the prince-bishops and Durham's reputation as a centre of pilgrimage, it is hardly surprising that the conquering Normans should wish to replace the Saxon cathedral with another which would reflect their authority and skill. The result was England's noblest piece of Norman architecture and the North's biggest building, begun in 1093 under the second Bishop, William of St Carileph.

The original Cathedral, perhaps the design of St Carileph himself, consisted of a triple-apsed east end, a choir of four bays, transepts, and a nave of eight bays (**12**), with two western towers. The Anglo-Norman stonemasons, numbering some 180 judging from masons' marks still visible in the triforium, and with experience of earlier churches in the South, worked at speed. At first, cut stone from the demolished Saxon church would have been available, although the supply of new stone was close at hand just off the Peninsula beyond South Street. In six years the choir aisles were enclosed and the high vault of the choir was constructed. The transepts followed, and in 1104 the shrine of St Cuthbert was placed behind the high altar in the central apse of

the new Cathedral. After 40 years, in 1133, the Cathedral was completed: the building that can be appreciated today.

The north door, the modern point of entry, was originally the entrance to the Cathedral for criminals seeking the right of sanctuary. (In his lifetime St Cuthbert had prophesied that his body would become a goal for 'fugitives and guilty men of all sort'.) It was marked by its medieval sanctuary knocker (**13**), now perhaps the most famous of its kind. The bronze head was probably cast in Durham around 1140. The powerfully grotesque monster, a refinement from cruder stone vaulting corbels, is made up of a flared lion's mane and pointed cat's ears, a long human nose, lined cheeks, and serrated teeth gripping the large handle or ring. With its original coloured glass or enamelled eyeballs, it must have presented the fugitive with a terrifying representation of both the power of the Church and the prospect of eternal damnation. Fascination has replaced fear today, and a replica has replaced the original, which was transferred to the Cathedral treasury in 1980 to preserve it from modern atmospheric pollution.

The great west door, now blocked, was the early point of entry. The impression the building would have made on medieval minds, attuned to

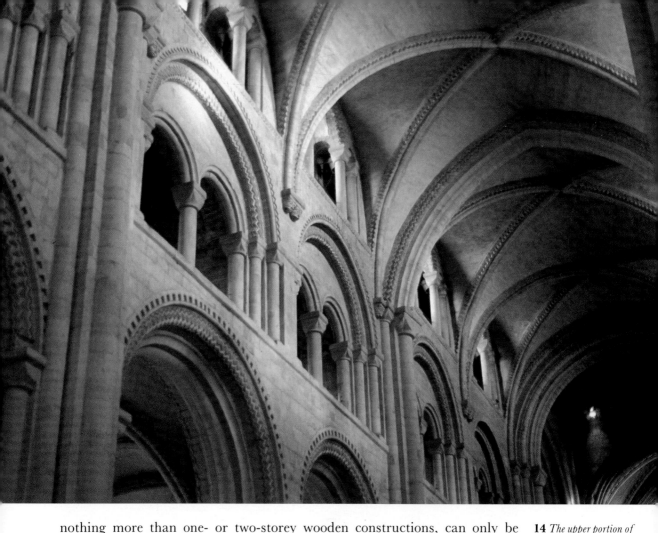

nothing more than one- or two-storey wooden constructions, can only be guessed. From the west door the nave extended for 200 feet, the whole building nearly double that figure. The ceiling soared 75 feet above and was built entirely of stone – this was the very first major building daring to span such wide spaces with anything but timber. The secret lay in arches, which acted as flying buttresses, thrown across the triforium between each bay. The stone ceiling is thus supported not only by intersecting barrel vaults, but by a series of heavy transverse arches rising from the massive composite pillars, which alternate with cylindrical pillars as round as they are high. The outline of the concealed, primitive buttresses can be glimpsed in the triforium above the side aisles when standing to one side of the nave. The geometry of the scientific construction providing the architectural significance of Durham is openly visible. Imagination is needed, however, to appreciate one further point of interest in the early church, namely, its decoration. We may accept the buff colour of the sandstone as natural and appropriate; indeed, in places the swirl of the sandstone grains is attractive in its own right. But as the small restored section on the south wall by the mutilated Neville tombs indicates, the original building would have been richly painted, probably in bold designs of red and black. There would also have been more coloured glass than at present.

The **Galilee Chapel** (**16**), entered by doors at either side of the great west portal, is a late 12th-century extension of the Cathedral to provide a Lady

14 The upper portion of the north side of the nave, showing the triforium, clerestory and distinctive early 12th-century ribbed vaulting.

15 The south side of the nave. The strength and verticality of the Cathedral is emphasised by the massive pillars, alternating between cylindrical columns, with distinctive chevron or diaper patterns, and compound piers whose engaged shafts soar to the transverse arches.

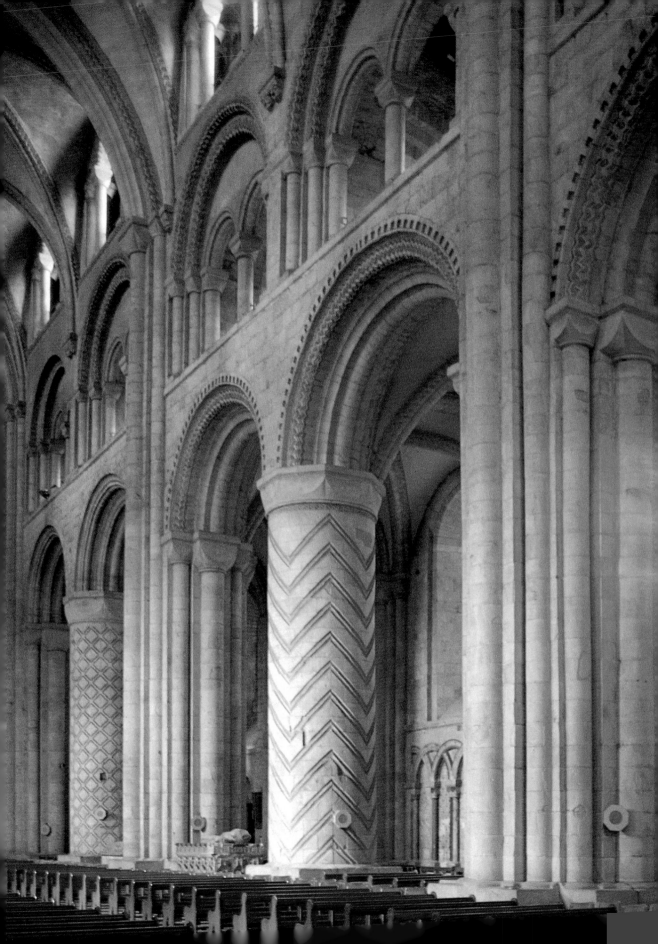

Chapel. The first attempts by Bishop Hugh le Puiset to erect one in the more usual location at the east end of the building had been thwarted by cracking walls. This was interpreted as a sign of displeasure, either of the Almighty, or of St Cuthbert, at the thought of having women so close to his shrine. (The rule of Durham was that women were not permitted beyond the two end bays of the nave. The delimitation of this zone is still marked by the line of black Frosterley marble across the back of the nave.) The Chapel was therefore transferred to the narrow space between the west end of the Cathedral and the near-precipitous gorge. The site determined its proportions – broad but with little depth. It was completed in 1175.

In the half-century following completion of the nave, the Romanesque style changed dramatically. To descend the steps from the nave into the Chapel is to pass from darkness to light, from the monumental to the delicate. Slender columns support arches highly decorated with dog's-tooth chevron mouldings. The chevron marking is sometimes taken to symbolise the waves on the Sea of Galilee; the Chapel's name, however, derives from the Sunday procession which ended here and which symbolised Christ's return to Galilee. The Chapel, like the nave, was originally brightly painted. Here, whole sections of the 12th-century wall paintings are still distinctly, if faintly, visible above the spandrels. More impressive are the original wall paintings of St Cuthbert (**17**) and St Oswald behind the north altar.

In front of the Chapel's central altar, which blocks the west door, is the tomb of Bishop Langley (1406–37), planned by himself. Bishop Langley altered the Chapel in various ways. He made the small entrances either side of the west door, provided a new roof, and doubled the shafts on the columns, adding two pillars of local sandstone to the original Purbeck marble. The different types of stone are evident from the subsequent erosion of the marble, caused unwittingly by the introduction of coke braziers. The massive outside buttresses which prevent the Galilee Chapel from slipping into the gorge are also the work of Bishop Langley. Their size is best appreciated from South Street; the precipitous nature of the gorge is evident from a glance through the two narrow windows at the back of the Chapel.

To the right of Langley's chantry is the simple, black, marble-topped tomb-chest of St Bede (**18**), or the Venerable Bede, as England's first man of letters is more often known. His remains were moved here in 1370, having previously been near to the shrine of St Cuthbert, and had their own gold and silver shrine until the Reformation. Some majesty was restored in 1970 with the erection on the east wall behind the tomb of the perforated oak screen with gilded aluminium lettering giving a quotation in Latin and English translation from the writings of Bede (*Christus est stella matutina*, 'Christ is the morning star'). Designed by George Pace as a memorial to Dean Alington (1933–51), it is best seen in the late afternoon, when sunlight and shadow add their own patterned beauty to the whole of the Chapel.

Another modern addition to the Chapel is the stained-glass window by Alan Younger, inserted in 1973 to commemorate the 1,300th anniversary of Bede's birth. Close scrutiny of the depicted scenes and styles sets Bede within the context of the transition of Christianity from the Celtic to the Latin tradition. Other windows contain many fragments of medieval glass, recently reinserted.

Following the extension of the west end of the Norman church, the 13th

16 The Galilee Chapel, situated at the west end of the Cathedral. Late Romanesque or Transitional in style, its lightness contrasts markedly with the nave, from which it is entered. The slenderness of the pillars was even more pronounced before the 15th century, when each of the twin Purbeck marble shafts was doubled with standstone pillars.

OVERLEAF

17 A section of the extensive late 12th-century wall painting in the Galilee Chapel. The figure of St Cuthbert is considered one of the finest wall paintings of its period in Europe.

18 The simple tomb-chest of the Venerable Bede (died AD 735) in the Galilee Chapel. Behind, on the east wall, is the gilded screen designed by George Pace.

19 *The rose window at the east end of the Cathedral, reconstructed by James Wyatt in the early 19th century.*

century saw the rebuilding and enlargement of the east end, for the original was showing signs of cracking. Perhaps equally important was the desire to provide a more spacious setting for the shrine and for the numerous pilgrims it attracted; there was also need for additional altars for the increased number of priests wishing to say Mass. Hence the Chapel of Nine Altars, planned by Bishop le Poor (1229–37) and built by Richard of Farnham. Bishop le Poor had previously been at Salisbury Cathedral, and evidently wished to introduce its Early English style to Durham.

During a fitful construction period lasting from 1242 until 1280, the apsidal ending was replaced by a T-shaped one. The form is that of an east transept, much wider and apparently higher than the main church. The chief impression is one of soaring height and space, an effect achieved by lowering the floor (this may have combated difficulties with the foundations at the same time) and by inserting tall lancet windows between fluted columns of alternating sandstone and Frosterley marble shafts. (The dark, polished marble, named after the village in upper Weardale, appears on close inspection to be almost as much fossil as metamorphosed limestone.) The slenderness is continued by the vaulting ribs. Aloft, the transverse ribs in the north and south bays are intriguingly on a skew to the central bosses. At ground level, the position of the original nine altars is clearly evident, set within the three large bays, each further subdivided into three.

The **rose window** (**19**), 90 feet in circumference, was first filled in the 15th century but was reconstructed by Wyatt in the early 19th century. A central Christ in Majesty is surrounded by the 12 apostles, with crowned elders from the Book of Revelation; on either side are two rows of Durham bishops, priors and deans.

The large north window, with its double layer of intersecting tracery, is considered the finest Gothic design in Durham. It is unique in the north of England. Its glass is 19th-century, as is most of that in the Chapel. The Chapel also contains the white statue by John Gibson of a pensively seated Bishop van Mildert (1826–36). He was the last Prince-Bishop and co-founder of the University along with Dean Thorp. In front of the statue is the simple slab marking the grave of the first burial allowed in the Cathedral, that of Bishop Anthony Bek (1284–1311).

A flight of steps leads to the feretory. Here, behind the high altar, were the holy relics of the medieval church and the ornate shrine of St Cuthbert (**20**). At the Reformation the relics were dispersed, the shrine was broken up and the saint was buried beneath a simple slab. The few loose stones are all that is left of the shrine. The present grey marble cover, with the single word 'Cuthbertus' inscribed, has a dignity which it is difficult to imagine the elaborate shrine ever possessed. Above, something of the previous colour has been reintroduced with the modern tester (**21**), depicting Christ in Glory surrounded by symbols of the four evangelists. Suspended from the vaulting, it hangs where the painted and gilded shrine cover would have been.

20 *St Cuthbert's tomb behind the high altar and Neville Screen. From 1104, when the body was translated to the new cathedral, until the Reformation, an ornate shrine occupied the space. A few stones remaining from its destruction surround the present marble slab.*

21 *The tester, or canopy, over St Cuthbert's tomb, designed by Sir Ninian Comper (1949). Its elaborate gilding is a modern echo of the richness of the medieval shrine.*

In 1829 the grave was opened up in an effort to solve conflicting traditions about the Reformation burial of St Cuthbert. The site was emphatically confirmed. The skeleton of the saint was found in the original decayed coffin, wrapped in linen and five layers of coloured and delicately patterned silk. A pectoral cross was on his chest. Other contents were a second skull, assumed to be that of King Oswald, and gifts given to the shrine by King Athelstan in 934. Many of the priceless finds are now displayed in the Cathedral Treasury.

The worn statue on the north side of the feretory is of St Cuthbert holding the head of King Oswald; it is probable that it was originally on the central tower. The curving black line on the paving marks the original east end of the Cathedral – the foundations are visible through the trap door – and indicates the scale of the 13th-century extension. In the opposite direction, the rear of the 14th-century Neville screen closes off the space from the high altar and choir.

In the choir the skeletal stone reredos, the **Neville screen (22)**, is an eye-catching focus. The delicate Perpendicular geometry is of Caen stone from Normandy, worked by Henry Yevele in London and given by John, Lord Neville. Dating from 1372 to 1380, it took a year to reassemble when it arrived in Durham. Among the pieces were 107 statues of various sizes which formerly filled the many niches. In the central niche stood a statue of the Virgin Mary, with St Cuthbert and St Oswald on either side. Unnecessary as it may seem to the modern eye, the attractive white stone was originally brightly painted. Perhaps an impression of the former colour may be gauged on the south side of the choir from the regilded altar tomb (**23**) of Bishop

22 *The 14th-century Neville Screen, the magnificent visual focus of the choir behind the high altar. The tall Perpendicular tracery, though deprived of its 107 alabaster statues at the Reformation, still shuts off the choir, visually and physically, from the tomb of St Cuthbert.*

24 *Part of the 17th-century wooden choir stalls, their tall canopies echoing the stone tracery of the Neville Screen.*

23 *Bishop Hatfield's chantry, or altar tomb, on the south side of the choir, with the episcopal throne above. Both were designed by Hatfield's chief mason, John Lewyn, about 1365-75.*

Hatfield (1345–81). The Bishop's throne above it is said to be the highest in Christendom. Both were designed by Bishop Hatfield himself.

The western half of the choir has dark, ornate choir stalls (**24**) with High Gothic canopies and fine misericords (the carved ledges under the seats which supported medieval choristers during the long services). They carry the distinctive signature of the first Restoration Bishop, John Cosin (1660–72), or, more specifically, that of the Bishop's craftsman, James Clement of Durham. The same exuberant woodwork once formed the choir screen, part of which now stands at the back of the south aisle, having been replaced by Sir George Gilbert Scott's marble screen in the 1870s. The tall font cover at the west end of the church is of the same pedigree. These examples represent the oldest woodwork in the Cathedral, since anything earlier was burnt by Scottish prisoners held captive in the Cathedral during the winter of 1650 after their defeat at Dunbar by Cromwell. The one exception is the clock of Prior Castell (1494–1519), which stands in the south transept, reputedly spared because it carries the emblem of the Scottish thistle. (Note the unusual division of minutes on the clock face.)

Above, the choir shows the clear but not discordant join between the Norman and Early English. The fifth bay, together with triforium and clerestory, was added to link the choir to the Chapel of Nine Altars and substituted the pointed for the rounded. An overall unity was achieved through the replacement of the vaulting for the whole choir. The original Norman vaulting, which was found to be in a dangerous condition by the

early 13th century, was taken down and reconstructed in the same style as that of the Nine Altars, with richly decorated vaulting ribs and transverse arches.

The Cathedral was built as an abbey-church. Access to the Benedictine Abbey or Monastery was through two doors at either end of the south aisle. Today the Monks' Door, retaining its original 12th-century timber and decorated ironwork and set within an ornamented Norman arch, is the doorway to the best-preserved monastery in the country. Entry is first to the cloisters, rebuilt by Bishop Skirlaw (1388–1405) and, apart from the timber ceiling and bosses, heavily restored in the early 19th century. The cloisters, once protected by glazing, were where much of the day-to-day work was performed. Peg marks for the monks' workbenches and cupboards can still be seen along the north cloister wall.

Off the west range of the dormitory undercroft is the spendiment (a medieval term for locked treasury), where the Cathedral's priceless ancient manuscripts are kept in temperature-controlled vaults. At the end of the range is the Cathedral treasury or museum (by Ian Curry, 1978) and a bookshop and restaurant (by George Pace, 1976). Above all three, running the length of the west range, is the **Monks' Dormitory** (**25**). Built by Bishop Skirlaw, it has one of the most remarkable wooden ceilings in the country. The original 40-foot baulk oak timbers, cut from the Abbey's nearby estate at Beaurepaire, still span the whole 200 feet of the hall floor. The position of the monks' cubicles can be gauged from the arrangement of the lower windows.

25 The original oak roof timbers of the former Monks' Dormitory, attached to the Cathedral. The Dormitory was constructed by Ellis Harpour for Bishop Skirlaw at the end of the 14th century.

26 A fragment of a cross-shaft from the collection of pre-Norman sculpture and casts housed in the Monks' Dormitory.

Today the room is a library of the Dean and Chapter and also houses a collection of pre-Conquest stone sculptures (**26**).

The Dean and Chapter's more valuable collection of early printed books is behind the south range in the former refectory, which was converted to a library in the 17th century. The desks for standing readers fit the dignified severity of both furniture and fenestration. Behind is the former Prior's Kitchen, considered one of the most remarkable monastic buildings in England. Designed and built by John Lewyn, (1366–74), it is an octagonal building with vaulting echoing that of a mosque, composed of eight intersecting semi-circular ribs, and a central octagonal louvre for ventilation and light. It only ceased being the Deanery kitchen in 1940; it is now the Muniment Room, housing the archives of the University's Department of Paleography and Diplomatic.

On the east side of the cloister is the polygonal Chapter House, completed by Bishop Rufus (1133–41) but half destroyed in 1796 during 'restorations' under Wyatt and rebuilt a century later by C. Hodgson-Fowler. Tombstones of some of the earliest bishops are set in the floor on the west side.

The wooden statue by Fenwick Lawson (1983) in front of the south range is of St Cuthbert, here shown in his favoured Farne Island setting. It was carved from an elm which grew for over two hundred years at the northern entrance to the Cathedral. From the statue there is a good view of the tall central tower, rebuilt in the 15th century after the previous smaller one was struck by lightning. Another point of interest here is the small area of patterned stonework on the south transept which escaped the severe chipping or scraping of the external stonework during the late 18th-century restoration.

27 *The south face of the Deanery from across the green of The College. Above its low roof rises the pinnacled transept of the Nine Altars.*

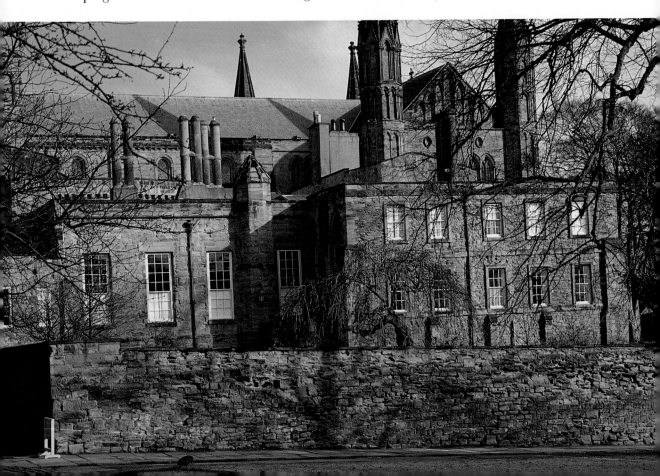

From the south-east corner of the cloisters, a dark echoing passage leads out into a delightful green close, which, with the surrounding buildings, is known as The College, after the college of canons. The varied stone buildings were all once part of the Monastery, with the **Deanery** (**27**), the former prior's lodging, being the largest and most intriguing: an architectural patchwork of the 13th and 14th centuries, with some Georgian restyling and an external stairway added by Pace in 1974, which is visible through his equally recent iron gateway in the high garden wall. Even the tall chimney stacks do not look out of place in the Deanery's make-up.

The south side of the green has a more uniform frontage, of apparently Georgian canons', or prebends', houses; medieval foundations and details abound behind. At the top end of the green is the Chorister School; boys scuttling to and fro wear the palatinate purple whether in school, choir or sports uniform. On the lawn nearby rises a squat, octagonal, stone water tower (**28**) – a gracious Georgian solution to a functional problem. A simpler boxed hand pump, a few yards away, formerly tapped one of the local water-tables of the Peninsula.

Near the bottom, or east end, of The College is the former Exchequer, set back, with twin extensions harbouring its own immaculate lawn. The different sets of fenestration do not detract from the successful 18th-century symmetry. Beware of attempting to capture perfection with the camera, however, for the spires of the Chapel of Nine Altars behind will attach themselves to the roof. Nearby is the early 16th-century gatehouse, with star-vaulting and bosses and, formerly, St Helen's Chapel above. The gatehouse is the link to the rest of the Peninsula and its massive gates are still bolted every evening at 10.30 pm to leave the modern-day community enclosed within its ancient bounds.

28 The mid-18th-century water tower, an elegant stone structure at the west end of The College. In the background the Cathedral and Deanery are seen across the green.

4 The Peninsula

The Peninsula constitutes the highly distinctive core of the city. The river-girt plateau originally provided a naturally defensive site which was reinforced before the arrival of the Normans by an enclosing earth rampart and timber palisade. Bishop Ralph Flambard (1099–1128) replaced the palisade with a stone wall, at the same time clearing the plateau of townspeople and resettling them in the shadow of the Castle so that the enclosed ecclesiastical and military community would 'neither be endangered by fire nor by filth'. Centuries later many of the properties lining the eastern side of the Peninsula became fashionable town houses. Today the whole area is largely shared between the Church and University.

The Cathedral's twin in this World Heritage Site, the Castle, presents a formidable defence of the northern approach to the Peninsula and is an obvious starting-point. Its plan consists of an eccentric keep on a mound (**29**) and a north and west range which, together with the barbicaned gate or gatehouse, encloses a triangular inner bailey. Beyond was originally a dry moat and an extended wall system.

The present architectural imprint of the Castle does not have the purity of innovative features evident in the Cathedral, but its Norman origins are impressively apparent. The building's variety is partly due to the fact that it was a home or palace as well as a castle. As its defensive role declined over the centuries, so alterations were made to provide gracious living-quarters for the prince-bishops. In 1837 the Castle was given to the newly founded University of Durham as its first college. The bishops henceforward lived permanently in the castle at Bishop Auckland, retaining the right to use the state rooms in Durham Castle.

Entry to the Castle is across the former dry moat and through the imposing gatehouse, originally the work of Bishop le Puiset and heavily 'restored' at the end of the 18th century by Wyatt, who 'romanticised' the upper storeys. The 16th-century heavy oak doors, with studded ironwork, give access to the inner bailey or courtyard (**30**). The elegance revealed is partly the result of 16th- to 18th-century façades or additions to the original ranges. The fenestration of the north range, straight ahead, is particularly deceptive, as can be seen from inside. In general terms, however, the octagonal keep is attributed to Bishop Flambard, rebuilt by Bishop Hatfield (1345–81), but ruinous again before a further rebuilding by Anthony Salvin (1840), this time for student accommodation. The north range is the work of Flambard and le Puiset, while the west range, incorporating the Great Hall, is that of Bishops Bek (1284–1311) and Hatfield. The two ranges remained separate buildings until Bishop Cosin joined them by means of a staircase enclosed within the corner tower. The main portico entrance in front of the west range is also attributable to Cosin; its nine steps are the invitation to a rich architectural and historical feast inside.

29 *The octagonal Norman keep of Durham Castle on its artificial mound forms a visual marker at the northern end of Palace Green.*

The Kitchen is reached after passing through a black door carved in deep relief, similar to the kind seen in the Cathedral. This door was in fact in the Cathedral as part of Cosin's choir screen until 1846. In the Castle it joined many other pieces of similar sumptuous woodwork commissioned by this first Restoration bishop. The Kitchen – formerly le Puiset's guardroom – and the Buttery are the work of Bishop Fox (1494–1501). The huge deep fireplaces, low stone arches and ancient brickwork with imitative castellation evoke grand medieval banquets (**31**). Many a monarch has been served from this kitchen on a scale to match the architecture: perhaps the prize goes to Margaret, daughter of Henry VII, who, on her way to marry James IV of Scotland, was entertained to a banquet which lasted for three days. Above the wooden serving hatches in the half-timbered Buttery is the date 1499 in Arabic figures and the motto of Bishop Fox, *Est Deo Gracia*, which was a blessing of the food as it passed on its way to the dining hall.

The Great Hall is here aptly named, 100 feet long and one of the grandest dining halls in the country. Its architecture is a historical mosaic: the original construction was by Bek; the timber roof was installed by Hatfield; the minstrels' galleries were added by Fox; the oldest windows are at the southern end of the Hall, while the great north window was inserted in the 19th century. The display of armour in the gallery dates largely from the 17th century and is a reminder that the prince-bishops were obliged to maintain their own military unit. The portraits are of University founders and benefactors and of subsequent masters of the College. The Hall is the annual setting for the degree-awarding ceremonies by the University's Chancellor, the finery of academic regalia being a modern evocation of past splendours when prince-bishops entertained nobility and royalty. A decided air of dignity pervades the room.

The Tunstall Gallery, reached by one flight of Cosin's staircase, has interesting furnishings and displays, but the eye is attracted to the Norman doorway, Durham's most magnificent (**32**). The three orders of columns and intricate ornamentation tell that it was originally the outside, ceremonial entrance to le Puiset's Hall, positioned exactly opposite the gatehouse. The Tunstall Gallery was later built in front of it and the doorway blocked up as the Hall behind was subdivided.

Le Puiset's Hall was converted into a series of well-appointed domestic apartments. Perhaps the most remarkable is the bishop's drawing-room, renamed the Senate Room when the University became the occupant. It is cocooned in 17th-century Flemish tapestries covering three of its walls, which have the acoustic effect of absorbing any sound as soon as it is uttered. On the fourth is a visual feast, the sumptuous overmantle, commemorating in its heraldic carving the visit of James I. The repetitions of the lion and the unicorn emphasise that James was the first monarch to use these emblems as supporters of the royal coat of arms, henceforward quartered into those of England and Scotland.

At the end of the Tunstall Gallery is the **Tunstall Chapel** (**33**), which replaced an original crypt chapel in 1542. Bishop Crewe (1674–1721) enlarged it eastward, the extension being visible in the change from fine ashlar blocks to rougher stone walls. A pleasing harmony was retained by reinstating the original east window. The carved oak return stalls at the west end were transferred from the Bishop's Chapel at Auckland Castle in the 16th

30 *The Castle courtyard, looking toward the west front, with the main entrance to its Great Hall (13th-14th century). The corner tower (on the right) houses the famous Black Staircase. The Castle is now occupied by University College.*

century. The misericords merit inspection, not least for their humorous depictions. Observe, for example, the protesting wife being wheeled away in a barrow.

The Black Staircase at the west end of the Tunstall Gallery is the finest of its kind in England. It is more than 7 feet wide on the lowest flight and rises altogether through a remarkable four floors around a square open well. Moreover, when first built by Cosin in 1662 it was bonded into the walls and thus free-standing. Later sagging in the well – suggesting an exaggerated postprandial experience – was caused by the weight of an extra room on the top storey and required the insertion of columns between the newel posts. The ornately carved balustrade panels are of painted pine.

The Norman Gallery is entered after ascending the Black Staircase. The heavy chevron friezes of the window arcading are a ready clue to the naming of this part of le Puiset's upper hall. The deep window bays of the triple arcading along the south range should be examined at close quarters to confirm that the outside fenestration is in fact 18th-century Gothic – seen earlier from the courtyard. The north range is currently student accommodation. The view westwards, over Framwellgate Bridge way below, must have assured early occupants of the impregnable nature of their Castle. All raids were indeed repulsed, but unfortunately the ravages of time took their toll of the building between the World Wars of the 20th century. Slippage into the river became a strong possibility and other walls began to lean – the south wall of the Norman Gallery leans 27 inches out of true – as the long-term

OVERLEAF

31 *A great late 15th-century castellated fireplace, one of three in the Castle kitchen. Where once great banquets were prepared, the demands of some 400 undergraduates of University College now have to be satisfied.*

32 *The finest Norman doorway in Durham. Originally the ceremonial entrance to le Puiset's Hall from the Castle courtyard, it now leads off the Tunstall Gallery to the Senate Room and Bishop's quarters.*

consequence of building the Castle on some 50 feet of unconsolidated sand and gravel. It took an international effort to finance the rescue of the building, by high-pressure pumping thousands of tons of cement to underpin the foundations and tying the walls. The task was spearheaded by Bishop Henson (1920–39) and generously supported by the Pilgrim Trust of America.

The **Norman Chapel** (**35**), reached by descending a narrow newel stair from the Gallery, dates from 1072 – the earliest Norman work in Durham. Six circular pillars support low vaulting over narrow central and side aisles. The capitals are carved with grotesque figures, plants and geometric designs; the columns exhibit a natural attraction in their own right with swirling grains of the colourful local sandstone. The floor is paved in a herringbone pattern, partly with original Norman flagstones. Long neglected or used for storage, the Crypt Chapel was restored as far as possible to its original condition in 1952. It constitutes an unforgettable architectural space, womb-like in conception, with remarkable acoustic qualities which can be experienced thrice weekly in the plainsong chant of Vespers, sung appropriately in medieval Latin.

There can be few more agreeable townscapes than that of Palace Green. Lined by historic buildings, with trees softening the foreground to the major edifices north and south, the whole ensemble is worth contemplating as an entity before focusing in more detail. The most obvious vista, if the approach has been up Owengate, is from the plinth commemorating the World Heritage designation south towards the Cathedral. Exposed to full view, the building is like a mighty ship at anchor. At night, with the foreground darkened and the Cathedral detailed by tungsten illumination, the experience is breathtaking. In noticing how none of the flanking buildings challenges the Cathedral, it is interesting to reflect that the multi-storey University Library was inserted at the south-west end in the 1960s. While clearly visible from South Street, from the Green it is quite hidden.

Bishop Cosin's Hall is the first prominent building on the left-hand or east side of the Green. Set back, the late 17th-century brick mansion, formerly an inn, takes its name from the years 1851–64 when it was a college of the University. It is now part of University College (the Castle). Its graceful proportions make its asymmetrically positioned doorway doubly puzzling to understand. The actual doorway, with pilasters and richly carved shell-hood, is eye-catching in its own right.

The long low building occupying the central position is known as **Bishop Cosin's Almshouses** (**34**). It was rebuilt in 1666 (see the tablet over the middle door), including Bishop Langley's earlier song and grammar schools at the two gable-end extremities. Now owned by the University, it houses the police office, a restaurant and a lecture room. Beyond the grey stone neo-Tudor Pemberton Building is the more elegant Queen Anne-style Abbey House, aptly occupied by the Department of Theology.

The west side of the Green is now largely lined by various sections of the University Library. The first building, next to the Castle's outer gate, is the Bishop's former Exchequer and Chancery (**36**). It was built in the mid-15th century by Bishop Neville, whose arms included a bull's head, which can be seen peering from the upper wall. The coat of arms of Bishop Cosin over the next building is yet one more example of the energy of this first Restoration

bishop. Here was a library for the public of the diocese. The collection contains Cosin's annotated copy of his suggestions for the 1662 Prayer Book. The University Library announces itself next. Built by Salvin in 1858 and considerably enlarged by Pace in 1968, it took on a more restricted role with the opening of the new University Library off the Peninsula in 1983. The castellated single-storey frontage of the former diocesan registry is separated by a vennel from the last building, the former grammar school, now the University Music Department. (Vennel, a Scottish word, is related to the French *venelle*, 'small street', from the Latin *vena*, 'vein'.)

The Bailey, North and South, forms another distinctive sub-unit on the Peninsula. Named after the multiple-enclosured defensive system, it runs the length of the Peninsula on the eastern side and parallel to the city wall, which lines the top of the river gorge in the gardens of properties facing the street. Many of the buildings on the sites of present houses originally belonged to the barons of the bishopric, who were responsible for the defence of the Castle. By the 15th century many of the houses had been sold to the Monastery; after the Reformation they became fashionable town houses for important country families and acquired their 18th- and 19th-century façades; today many of them accommodate colleges or departments of the University. The antiquity of their foundations is indicated by ground floors below the level of the street, which has been built up over the centuries.

Until 1820 the North Bailey began at the Great North Gate, which guarded the main entrance through the perimeter wall to the enclosed Peninsula. The imprint of the Gate is still evident in the steep incline at the head of Saddler Street, which is largely attributable to the subterranean remains of the Gate's

35 *The Norman or Crypt Chapel, the earliest Norman work surviving in Durham. Embedded deep in the Castle's foundations, it is an architectural gem with remarkable acoustical qualities.*

34 *Bishop Cosin's Almshouses on Palace Green, rebuilt by Cosin in 1668 and now part of the University.*

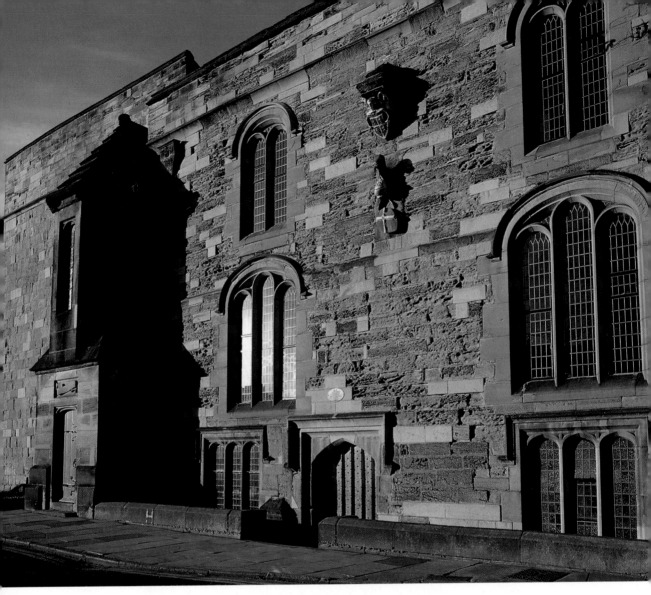

foundations. Above ground, a 13th-century bastion and part of the wall, connecting the keep to the Gate, is visible through the grille in the lower doorway of No. 50 Saddler Street.

36 *Bishop Neville's Exchequer Building (c. 1450), marked by the Neville coat of arms, on Palace Green, now forms part of the University Library.*

At the foot of Owengate, at the junction with the Bailey and Saddler Street, the pilgrim catches the first beckoning vision of the Cathedral's west towers. The glimpse is enriched by the gentle curve in the cobbled rise, lined by one of the city's few exposed-timber-framed dwellings. Owengate House, a classical early 19th-century building, was formerly a Victorian subscription library, as a fading inscription over the corner doorway reveals. Opposite is Halmote Court, rebuilt in 1850, a manorial court which dealt with minor offences. When it closed in 1952, it was the last of its kind in England. It is now appropriately the University Department of Law. Corbel heads of a king and a judge flank the door.

The shell-hood doorway of No. 5 North Bailey aptly marks the former home of Ignatius Bonomi (1797–1850), an eminent Durham architect who was also consultant to the Cathedral and county bridge surveyor. One hundred yards further on, the street line is broken by the entrance and forecourt of Hatfield College, the second oldest college in the University (1846) and originally intended for poorer students, providing furnished accommodation and communal eating – the universal pattern of today but unprecedented then. Incorporated within its buildings are parts of a mid-18th-century coaching inn, the Red Lion. The hostelry's assembly room is now the College Dining Room and the card room, the Senior Common Room. Its Chapel was built in 1853.

St Mary-le-Bow Church derives its name from the arch or bow which formerly spanned the North Bailey as part of a gate in the inner defences of the Peninsula. Both arch and tower collapsed in 1637, destroying much of the church's nave at the same time. The nave was rebuilt in 1683, the tower in 1702, and St Mary-le-Bow resumed its role as the parish church for the northern part of the Peninsula. It is thought to have been the site of the wattle church in which the coffin of St Cuthbert rested when first brought to Durham. The building is now a Heritage Centre.

Leading off the Bailey at this point are the cobbled streets of Bow Lane and Dun Cow Lane (**37**). Into the former protrudes a large Roman Doric portico marking the entrance to an 18th-century brick mansion, now part of Hatfield College. From the latter one is overwhelmed by the soaring height of the pinnacles of the Chapel of Nine Altars and central tower of the Cathedral. The lane was named at the renewal of the carving of the dun cow on the outside of the Chapel of Nine Altars around 1800; it was formerly known as Lyegate.

Opposite the Chapel of Nine Altars and the green with the First World War memorial is a range of buildings now belonging to St Chad's College. At the junction with Bow Lane a neo-Georgian dining room has been skilfully attached, built by Francis Johnson in 1961. Humour is allied to skill if you can see the gently bowed front as a bishop's mitre, for at the time the College was primarily for ordinands of High Church persuasion.

The buildings further south on the right are used as garages and offices by the Dean and Chapter, which body, as successor to the former Abbey, has a variety of estates and buildings to oversee. Their stonemason's yard is hidden behind the arched double gate. Standing on the nearby old mounting block will fail to give the inquisitive a view over the wall into the yard, but the decapitated lamp-post might offer a better aid. In any event, notice the inscription on the post: its former illumination was powered by sewer gas.

The South Bailey begins at the gateway to The College, and soon becomes intriguingly sinuous and surfaced with river-washed cobbles. Many of the former town houses now belong to St John's College. No. 3, Haughton House, built in 1730 by Sir Robert Eden, is the grandest, an impressive entrance to The College. No. 4, adjacent, is a late 17th-century amalgamation of several earlier units. It was the town house of the Bowes family, one of whom married the Earl of Strathmore and thus became an ancestor of the present royal family. Later owners were the Liddell family, ancestors of the Alice on whom Lewis Carroll's character was based. A glimpse of the gracious past is visible inside the first-floor drawing-room, the Tristram Room, named after the last occupants before the house became College property.

The little Church of St Mary-the-Less attempts to gain added stature from its elevated garth but is reduced to cosy Norman and put into context by the nearby mature beech and the view of the Cathedral tower behind. Once the

parish church for the southern half of the Peninsula, it is now the chapel for St John's College. The first church was erected in the 12th century but the present building dates from 1847, hence its immaculate order. There are a few authentic Norman remains – most noticeably, on the north wall of the chancel, an early 12th-century stone relief of Christ in Glory, which was originally in St Giles' Church. There is also a wall memorial to Count Boruwlaski, a 19th-century parishioner notable for his diminutive stature (39 inches tall), perhaps not inappropriate for such a small church.

The cobbled street gives a final twist, past the Dean and Chapter's nursery for the River Banks and another exuberantly moulded shell-hood doorpiece – now the entrance to St Cuthbert's Society of the University – before leaving the enclosed Peninsula through the Water Gate. The present opening is an enlargement of the former postern gate and was designed to allow carriages access to the new Prebends' Bridge, which was constructed at the same time (1778). The stray masonry either side of the top of the archway is said to be pieces of the Cathedral rose window discarded during Wyatt's reconstruction.

37 *(Above) Bow Lane, leading from Kingsgate Bridge to the Bailey, is named after St Mary-le-Bow Church, which stands in the shadow of the Cathedral. (Right) Former town residences, now University properties: above, 100 Dun Cow Lane, leading to Palace Green; below, 93 The South Bailey as it approaches Watergate.*

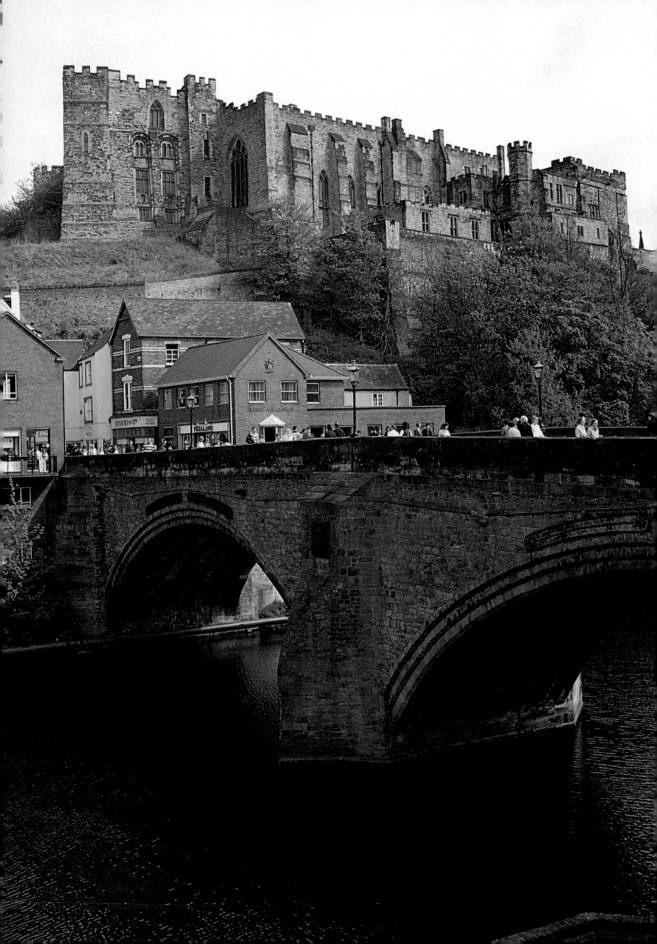

5 The River Banks

The River Banks are one of the glories of Durham. A tree-lined gorge, extending between the medieval bridges of Elvet (**39**) and Framwellgate (**38**), provides a green collar to the Peninsula. There is an ever-changing vista from the riverside paths, which are continuous around the inner bank of the meander loop and exist for most of the way on the outer bank.

The gorge itself is cut into a succession of sandstone, shale and thin coal seams, all of the Carboniferous age. The lip of most of the gorge is formed of Low Main Post Sandstone, sometimes called Cathedral Sandstone since the rock provided readily available building material for the Cathedral (and Castle). The reason why the river took a backward loop through solid rock in post-glacial times, rather than continuing to etch out a course in the soft fluvio-glacial sands and gravels which occupy its former broad valley, remains a mystery. It puzzled Leland on his visit in the 1530s:

> Some hold opinion, that of ancient tyme, [the River] Were [Wear] ran from the place wher now Elvet bridge is, straite down by St Nicholas, now standing on a hille; and that the other course, part for policy, and part by digging of stones for building of the towne and minstre, was made a valley, and so the water course was conveyed that way, but I approve not full this conjecture.

The legend may have had its origin in the fact that the earliest working of stone was probably in the gorge itself by Kingsgate Bridge. Other earlier workings were the Sacristan's Quarry in the Dell near Prebends' Bridge and below South Street, while the section between Cathedral and Castle known as Broken Walls is thought to derive its name from quarrying having encroached too close to the defences.

Elvet Bridge is at the beginning of the river loop around the Peninsula. Its slightly pointed arches carry a steeply rising carriageway into the raised Peninsula. Leland mentioned 14 arches; today ten are visible. Bishop le Puiset built the bridge in 1160 and it was repaired by Bishop Fox (1494–1501) in 1495. In the great storm of 1771, which left no bridge on the Wear untouched, the three central arches were destroyed. In 1804–5 the bridge was doubled in width on the upstream side. Le Puiset's work is still visible between the more modern ribs under all but the central arches on the downstream side. The numbers painted just above water level on the two central piers are for the guidance of rowing crews, a reminder that England's oldest rowing regatta is held here every June. The first was reputedly staged in 1815 to celebrate the victory at Waterloo, and the annual event is recorded officially as beginning in 1834.

There was originally a chapel at either end of the bridge. St Andrew's Chapel, at the lower end, is now marked by a Dutch-gabled shop at street

38 Medieval Framwellgate Bridge, with Durham Castle rising behind. A gatehouse formerly stood at the far end of the bridge, adding to the defence of the city.

level; on a pier below, some carving is visible of a bridge land arch. At the peninsular end of the bridge St James's Chapel had given way to a house of correction by the 17th century. Traces of the cells, in use until 1819, can be seen at the bottom of the steps under the uppermost visible land arch. You may also hear the ghostly piping of James Allen, which is said to haunt the cells. A gypsy piper imprisoned for horse-stealing, he died the day before his pardon arrived.

The riverside path linking Elvet to Kingsgate Bridge downstream, named Fearon Walk after a former headmaster of Durham School, clings to the steep peninsular bank while affording views opposite of three modern University buildings. Elvet Riverside 1 and 2 (built 1966 and 1975 respectively) both house Arts departments. Dunelm House (1965), to be seen in conjunction with the adjacent **Kingsgate Bridge** (**40**), is a bold modern inset, the only example of Brutalist style in Durham. The design of staggered cubes in

39 *Elvet Bridge, still incorporating some of its original 12th-century work, at the point where the river makes a right-angled turn to take a loop around the Peninsula. The Castle keep rises commandingly above the city.*

40 *The slender construction of Ove Arup's Kingsgate Bridge (1963), spanning the river at the site of an early ford.*

shuttered concrete, standing guard at the entrance to the gorge section of the river, won R.I.B.A. and Civic Trust Awards for its architect Michael Powers. Inside the building, which functions as a students' union and staff club, the same concrete finish provides a harsh environment, although relief is offered by the views out to the river, foliage and Cathedral.

Kingsgate Bridge is on the site of a ford below the city gate of that name. The king was William I, who is reported to have hastily left Durham this way, having been overcome with fear while plotting to open Cuthbert's coffin. The present bridge, which provides an essential link between separate parts of the University, was completed in 1963 and was also a Civic Trust award-winner. The slim high-level footbridge, supported by V-shaped struts, echoes in concrete the high-ribbed vaulting of the Cathedral. It was constructed in two halves, one on each bank, and then swivelled on its two bases across the river to complete the design. The structural designer was Ove Arup who, although better known for his work elsewhere (for example the Sydney Opera House), considered Kingsgate Bridge his favourite piece. In recognition, on the day of Sir Ove's funeral in 1988, members of each of his 15 offices placed wreaths on the bridge to commemorate their master's masterpiece.

The visitor now has a choice of continuing on the present footpath or ascending the steps to cross Kingsgate Bridge and turning right briefly into

42 *Resurrected victims of Dutch elm disease on the River Banks: when viewed from one particular spot the tree-trunks of Colin Wilbourn's 'The Upper Room' compose into the scene of the Last Supper.*

41 *The River Banks in winter. Seemingly in the depths of the country, the walk at the foot of the Peninsula is actually in the middle of the city.*

Church Street before taking the path across a churchyard to join the river path high on the outer bank. On this latter route, behind the west end of St Oswald's Church and just below the path, is St Oswald's Well. This is one of four wells or springs around the Banks, each attributable to the gentle gradient and juxtaposition of bands of pervious sandstone with impervious shale and coal. Access to this particular well is difficult and unsignposted. Onwards, the main path gently descends, passing the outlet of an air shaft from a former colliery and two streams, round towards Prebends' Bridge.

The path along the inner bank continues past two college boathouses before reaching Count's Corner, named after the Polish dwarf, Count Boruwlaski, who is commemorated in St Mary-the-Less. The 19th-century personality lived in a house – now demolished – some 100 yards nearer Prebends' Bridge than the present diminutive building known as the Count's House. The present empty shell, with a Greek Doric temple portico and dating from the 1820s, was in fact a summer house of a property in the South Bailey.

The pleasant glade on the inner loop of the river, a favourite picnic spot and the scene of students' summer open-air productions of Shakespeare, has recently acquired an intriguing sculpture. Towards the north end of the open expanse of grass are assembled the upright, shaven trunks of 13 trees which formerly grew on the Banks before becoming victims of Dutch elm disease (**42**). They were brought back to life by Colin Wilbourn during his time as Cathedral artist-in-residence (1988–9). In fact, the 'Upper Room' comes alive for each observer as he or she mounts the end seat within the enclosing elms. It is a *trompe-l'œil* highly appropriate for a city where mystery and surprise are pervasive qualities.

The three high, semi-circular arches and balustrated parapet of dignified **Prebends' Bridge** (**43**) span the Wear as soon as the river is clear of the southern loop. The bridge was built (1772–8) by George Nicholson, architect to the Dean and Chapter, and named after the prebends or canons of the Cathedral. (Vehicular traffic is restricted to that of the Dean and Chapter.) An earlier footbridge existed from the mid-16th century some 50 yards upstream; the stone abutment on the outer bank can still be seen. When it was washed away in the 1771 flood, the opportunity was taken to re-site it in order to open up the classic view and climax of any perambulation of the River Banks, an activity then highly in vogue. Visiting painters have all included at least one work from this particular viewpoint, including Edwards, Grimm, Hearne, Girtin, Vaughan, Daniell, Robson and, especially, Turner, whose painting captures supremely the sense of place, the *genius loci* of Durham. He turned the Cathedral almost 45° from its position astride the Peninsula, and in the ethereal colouring of the evening light it appears to be rising from the rock on which it is set. The contrived lines of the left-hand trees (cited by Ruskin as among the finest in all painting), distant bridge, weir and Prebends' Bridge parapet all lead the eye to the three towers to complete the spiritual symbolism of the picture. The poetry of this scene eludes the modern camera, however accurate the photographic record. That does not stop us from lining up beside the plaque with the well-known lines from Scott's 'Harold the Dauntless' in order to capture the wonderful view.

It is from the bridge that we can perhaps best reflect on the sylvan scene, apparently so natural yet very much a cultivated landscape. The Dean and Chapter have been landscape gardeners for well over two centuries. Trees and

43 *One of Durham's finest views: the southern approach to 18th-century Prebends' Bridge from the footpath on the south-western edge of the River Banks.*

bushes have been planted, pruned and occasionally felled – the peninsular slope was originally treeless for reasons of defence – flowers planted and grass mown, crushed dolomite paths laid out, seats provided and litter collected daily. The frequent change of prospect beside 'the best of all little rivers' led the American novelist, Nathaniel Hawthorne, and his wife to believe they were 'getting into the country', until the reappearance of the Cathedral made them realise they 'had made a circuit without our knowing it'.

Before leaving the bridge, two sensitivities of modern planning may be noticed. One is the siting of the four-lane Millburngate Bridge behind the medieval Framwellgate Bridge, which is restricted to pedestrians. Only a single concrete pier of the new bridge is visible. The other is the absence of development on the green skyline, so that the impression is given of looking to the heart of the city and beyond to the countryside.

On the west side of the bridge, in addition to the riverside path, there is a choice of ascending either directly to the White Gates and Quarry Heads Lane or diagonally to South Street. Ahead, on the former ascent, the arched brick feature conceals a drainage tunnel to a former mine, a reminder that the whole area is underlain by subterranean coal workings. In fact, on the wooded high ground around the southern lip of the gorge two capped shafts of 18th-century mines can be seen. At the beginning of the ascent to South Street a spring, known as South Spring Well, has been encased in simple fashion.

The riverside path brings the visitor to the pink mill or corn mill (**44**) which, with the old fulling mill opposite, originally belonged to the prior; the bishop's mill was further downstream. While the corn mill huddles in the shelter of the luxuriant tree cover, the mill opposite, with 17th-century stone walls and a pantile roof edged with stone slates, is more prominent (it is now a museum of archaeology). The eye is drawn to this focal point by the line of water breaking over the weir which, running diagonally between the two banks, enhances the stature of the river from modest to mighty at this point. Inevitably the composition is reordered and the mill reduced to domestic scale, not by the river but by the Cathedral, rising above the greenery to complete another famous view.

On the peninsular side of Prebends' Bridge there is also a choice of paths – through the Water Gate to the Bailey or rising gently in the shadow of the city wall, as well as the river path which leads to the fulling mill. At the junction of the latter two paths is the lamp-post – or its successor – which, it is said, inspired C.S. Lewis to mark the entrance to his mythical world of Narnia.

After the ascent, the path levels out at the foot of the former Abbey buildings and Galilee Chapel. There are views down to the former corn mill and across to the colourful and varied row of houses lining South Street. Two more wells are passed. One, the Galilee, is no longer accessible, its flight of steps being blocked; the other, St Cuthbert's, has recently become accessible again with the uncovering of the stone staircase and relaying of pavement. The stonework over the well has a 17th-century inscription; the spring itself has been intermittent since the strata were breached by foundations for the new University Library. At the point of descent, note the protruding rock outcrop on which the Cathedral is founded. Just before the outcrop the size of the 15th-century buttresses to the Galilee Chapel can be appreciated at close quarters.

Beside the vennel and former gate of Windy Gap, which gives access to Palace Green, is George Pace's Civic Trust award-winning extension to the University Library. Here its size can be appreciated for the first time, and the quality of its stone-faced finish.

The path now descends to Framwellgate Bridge. Its two wide elliptical arches carry Durham's first river crossing, built by Bishop Flambard in 1128. Rebuilding was undertaken after 1401 and widening in 1856, but some of the original construction is still visible on the downstream face. The gatehouse which guarded the peninsular end of the bridge was demolished in 1760. The contrasting views up- and downstream reveal clearly that the bridge was positioned at the junction of the gorge with the plain section of the river valley. As such, it marks the end of the Banks section which we have been following.

CHARLES WILLIAM VANE STEWART
3RD MARQUIS OF LONDONDERRY
1ST EARL VANE AND BARON STEWART
OF STEWARTS COURT K.G.G.C.B.
LORD LIEUTENANT COUNTY OF DURHAM

6 The City Centre

The Market Place, the civic and commercial centre of the city, grew in the shadow of the ecclesiastical-cum-military heartland on the Peninsula. Its complementary role was carefully overseen for several centuries by the Church authorities, even though the first charter was granted by Bishop le Puiset as early as 1179. Appropriately, therefore, the present-day architecture of the square exhibits a certain modesty: there is no attempt at the grandeur which a cathedral city might be expected to display at its civic focus. The Market Place nevertheless has a dignified coherence, which stems from extensive mid-19th-century rebuilding and from sandblasting and floor-scaping in the 1970s.

The Town Hall complex initiated the rebuilding. Erected in 1851 by public subscription and designed by P.C. Hardwick, it consists of the **Guildhall** (**46**), with a Perpendicular symmetry of three Tudor-arched doorways, balcony, large windows and central gable, and the Town Hall behind. The first Guildhall was erected in the 14th century for the guilds controlling the city's trade and commerce; it was rebuilt by Bishop Cosin in 1665, and much of his interior work was retained in the 19th-century rebuilding. The Town Hall has more than a hint of Parliament's Westminster Hall about it, with a large hammerbeam roof, stained glass depicting local history, heraldic panelling and a list of freemen. In the entrance hall is a copy of the 1179 charter and a life-size statue of Count Boruwlaski, with a showcase of his clothes and violin. The 39-inch Pole is certainly well remembered in his adopted city. To the left of the Guildhall is the entrance to the New Markets, completed in 1852 as part of the stone complex and providing a fascinating covered market; its varied stalls complement those erected weekly in the square.

St Nicholas' Church occupies the north side of the square. A Norman church and churchyard stood here until the 19th century. F.J. Pritchett's neo-Gothic replacement, completed in 1855, was surmounted by Durham's first spire. It is worth stepping through the door to see how Pritchett's interior has been imaginatively and colourfully converted (by R. Sim, 1981) to flexible use for 'seven whole days, not one in seven'.

45 *The electroplated statue of Lord Londonderry by Raffaelle Monti (1858). The City Council commissioned the statue, but on realising its size tried unsuccessfully to persuade the University to erect it on Palace Green. The third Marquess of Londonderry was a prominent 19th-century entrepreneur in the County's coal industry.*

Three banks continue the dignity on the other sides of the square, most notably the neo-classical National Westminster (J. Gibson, 1876) and neo-Gothic Barclays (A. Waterhouse, 1887). Quoined Georgian houses complete the sympathetic infilling along with one department store – and even this 1930s example of art deco respects the ambience of the place. The central feature is the equestrian statue of the third Marquess of Londonderry (**45**), a leading 19th-century coal-owner and political figure in the county. His hussar uniform reflects his earlier career as a successful soldier who served with Wellington. The sculpture, completed by R. Monti in 1861, is one of the first examples of the use of electroplating. Today the visual prominence of the composition is almost overwhelming from certain positions in the modest Market Place.

Less dominant in architectural terms, but equally determined in posture, is the elevated figure of Neptune nearby. The statue was originally the gift of John Bowes, a prominent local landowner and one of a group of entrepreneurs seeking in the 1720s to make Durham a seaport through improving the navigation of the Wear. The project failed, but the statue remained, placed on top of the Market Place Pant, which was the only public supply of water until the mid-19th century. (A conduit had been brought from Fram Well-head, on the other side of the river, in 1450.) Statue and Pant were removed in 1923 in deference to increasing vehicular traffic, Neptune being re-erected in Wharton Park. The advent of pedestrianism in 1976 made possible his return; it was achieved in 1991 after a campaign by the City of Durham Trust, the local civic amenity society.

Before leaving the Market Place one should reflect on two points of detail in its history. One is the former police-box which eventually replaced Neptune and had the task of controlling the three converging streams of traffic until pedestrianisation. Before the advent of related traffic lights and a unique television monitor, wholesale destruction of properties in narrow Silver Street was seriously considered in order to give priority to motorised vehicles.

The second point of interest is that the square once marked the northernmost extension of the city wall. In the compact area enclosed within the enlarged circuit of 1314, the north wall of St Nicholas' Church was actually part of the fortification, together with a gate, Clayport, guarding the entry from Claypath. The gate was demolished in 1791. Historically, then, the civic focus, at the meeting point of three narrow winding streets, was more confined than the present enclosed space. Further exploration of today's city centre continues along each of these streets.

Claypath leads northwards out of the Market Place and immediately on to an overpass. The location is noisy, but the prospect allows the visitor to make sense of part of the puzzling map of Durham. The River Wear can be seen east and west, coming to within 250 yards of severing the Peninsula, which it forms by its horseshoe course around the Cathedral. The peninsular neck was in fact severed, and the continuous building line of Claypath broken, by the Leazes Road by-pass (1967); together with the new Elvet Bridge (1975), it freed the central streets of traffic. The Cathedral car-park (William Whitfield, 1975, R.I.B.A. commendation) is a civilised solution to the stacking of vehicles. Its brickwork evokes the role of the city wall which formerly linked with Clayport Gate. On the opposite side, the open area is awaiting reinstatement of the building line in a scheme which will incorporate the site of the former and famous Durham Carpet Factory, which moved to the eastern outskirts of the city in the 1970s.

The corrugated building to the west, opposite Millburngate House, is the fun palace housing Durham's ice rink. A local refrigerator firm laid out a rink in 1939, and during the Second World War Canadian airmen stationed in the vicinity took the first hockey sticks on to the ice. From these beginnings has evolved one of the country's leading ice-hockey teams. A link with more ancient history can be seen in the mill race, formerly serving the bishop's mill, which generates electricity to help produce the ice for the rink.

A journey up Claypath, past the United Reform (formerly Congregational) Church crowned with a stocky spire (H.T. Gradon, 1888), is rewarded by the visual delight of Leazes Place to the east. Two identical rows of dark brick

66

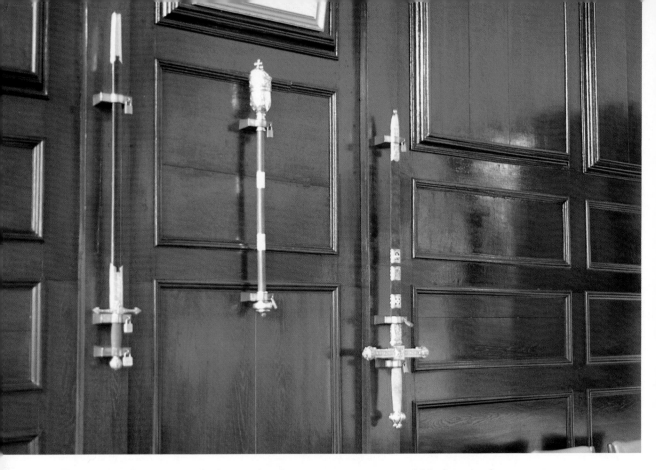

Regency-style terraces, facing each other across a narrow cobbled street, have the appearance of a theatre set. They formed Durham's first planned street, built in 1846.

The second street leaving the Market Place, **Silver Street** (**49**), leads to Framwellgate Bridge. Winding and descending, it is Durham's most attractive shopping street, although much civic planners' time is spent preventing retailers from updating fascias in ever-louder idiosyncratic fashion. It is perhaps in Silver Street that the city's floorscaping scheme (1975–8, Civic Trust Award) can be best appreciated. While the treatment in most towns might more accurately be described as 'floor-slabbing', perhaps with seats and greenery added, here the use of second-hand York paving, granite setts and central wheelers has retained the linear nature of the street. The effect is both to give an attractive coherence to the townscape and to evoke a sense of the past. In this respect, the restored timber-framed premises of No. 32 look most at home. The adjacent vennel is one of three in the street; two lead steeply up to Moatside Lane, which yields close-up views alongside the castle mound as well as unglamorous glimpses of the irregular backs of Silver Street premises which are so colourful from the front. Happily, the same cannot be said of Back Silver Street, seen either from the vennel of that name or at a distance from across the river. Here, the backs of properties cascading in irregular fashion to the riverside play a critical supportive role in the general view of Castle and Cathedral. Modern additions acknowledge that these are properties with two frontages, most notably the extension of the premises of W.H. Smith back from the Market Place as it telescopes towards the river.

47 The city's ceremonial mace and swords in the Guildhall.

Millburngate Shopping Centre, occupying the river frontage between Framwellgate and Millburngate Bridges, has taken the shops inside, in the same way that the original Mill Burn is now confined to a conduit beneath North Road before emptying into the river by the weir. The Centre was built in two stages and came from the drawing-board of Building Design Partnership. The first, nearer to Framwellgate Bridge, is tied into the bridgehead. It echoes river maisonettes previously on the site and breaks up 68,000 square feet of shopping space in the interplay of brick and slated roofscape. The design earned Civic Trust and Europa Nostra Awards in 1978 and was featured on a British postage stamp. The second stage is less successful. Excessive angularity in essentially the same materials, together with a ponderous advance to the waterfront edge, has produced overall an extensive bulk which is contrary to the Durham idiom of physical diversity and varied age. The prime culprit in this respect, however, is Millburngate House on the other side of Millburngate Bridge. Completed in 1969 to house one-third of a million square feet of office space for the National Savings Certificate Division decentralised from London, its exterior of acid-washed, precast concrete units with strips and panels of grey aggregate bands yields not a jot to its setting. Perhaps we should be thankful that floor-to-ceiling measurements are at a minimum, thereby reducing overall height, also that a 16-storey tower was omitted. Actually, our gratitude should be directed to Thomas Sharp, for it was his intervention that caused the modifications to T.F. Winterburn's design. (It also cost him his consultancy post with the city.)

South Street must be on everyone's itinerary. The narrow street clings to the eastern edge of the river gorge as it rises sharply from Framwellgate Bridge; it formerly continued along the riverside towards Newcastle through the site now occupied by the Millburngate Centre. (The present North Road, leading directly from the bridge to the rail and bus stations, and the obvious modern entry for so many, was not constructed until 1831.) At the junction of steep South Street and even steeper Crossgate sits the compact Church of St

48 The Mayor's Chamber in the Town Hall dates from the rebuilding by Bishop Cosin in 1665, with 'modernisation' by George Bowes, who was responsible for the panelling. The painting to the left of the mayor's chair is of Bishop Lord Crewe, who granted a citizen's charter in 1685.

Margaret of Antioch, with a modest tower. It was founded as a chapel in the parish of St Oswald's, and inside the building's Norman origins are evident: the nave arcading on the south side is dated 1150, that on the north, along with the chancel, 1195. In the central aisle is a large, dark stone memorial to Durham's 17th-century equivalent of Dick Whittington and his wife. John Duck came to Durham seeking to become a butcher's apprentice but was refused membership of the guild. The fortune of the despondent youth changed when a gold sovereign was dropped at his feet by a raven. He became a wealthy butcher and coal-owner, was elected Mayor of the city and was knighted by Charles II. His impressive town house in Silver Street survived until the 1960s.

South Street begins with St Margaret's on one side and the flat-roofed public library (D. Cuthbertson, 1961) squatting below street level on the other. The succeeding terrace of new town houses, Dunelm Court (R. Gazzard, A. Burns, 1979), is not to be overlooked. Deliberately 'safe' rather than innovatory, the brick and stucco units incorporate several of the vernacular architecture elements found higher up the street. The earlier houses, as they ascend the street, present a colourful collection of 18th- and 19th-century façades, no two alike and none, considered in isolation, outstanding architecturally (**50**). Collectively, however, they constitute a highly attractive townscape, while opposite, across the gorge, is the theatre of the sublime. Standing near to the top of South Street the observer has the incomparable panorama of the Cathedral, its former Abbey buildings, the Castle, the spire of St Nicholas in the Market Place and, away northwards, the green Wear Valley. Durham is encapsulated in this view.

The third and last of the streets leaving the Market Place is Saddler Street,

49 Silver Street, leading from the Market Place to Framwellgate Bridge: the city's most attractive shopping street. It is difficult now to imagine that up to the late 1970s double-decker buses traversed this narrow and precipitous street.

50 *Some of the Georgian vernacular house-fronts near the top of South Street. They have an unimpeded view across the river gorge to the Cathedral (see overleaf). Early in its history this narrow street was briefly part of the Great North Road.*

which leads to Palace Green and Elvet Bridge. The first 50 yards is known as Fleshergate, which indicates it was once the butchers' quarter, but no evidence other than the name remains. The three- and four-storey 18th-century brick frontages on the west mask several timber-framed constructions (**52**). Most notable is No. 79, the probable residence of Sir Richard Saddler in the 16th century, which has a fine staircase and ornamental plaster ceiling on the second floor dating from this time. Behind No. 73, the building with a copper tea-pot, a trade sign for a grocer, was the country's first mustard factory. Here Mrs Clemens ground the first Durham Mustard in a small mill at the rear in the early 18th century; the business subsequently passed to Ainsley's before being bought by Coleman's of Norwich at the beginning of the 20th century.

The street divides at Magdalen Steps, as Saddler Street begins its rise towards Palace Green. One or two of the properties on either side of this last stretch are of particular interest. On the east side the attractively gabled Nos. 34–5 was the Beehive Inn in the early 18th century, when the street was noted for its theatres. The vennel on the left, with steep steps down to the river, bears the name of Drury Lane, recalling the theatre which adjoined it in the 18th century. The former box office and foyer are incorporated in the elegant double-fronted premises of Nos. 43–4. Its Greek Doric columns and bowed windows with examples of ancient glass today constitute the city's oldest shop front. In the 18th century another theatre was opposite, behind No. 61. The

71

frontage of this and the adjacent buildings is worth a glance, for in 1955 four properties were temporarily dismantled to provide rear access in order to erect Moatside Court as student accommodation for University College (architect, Bernard Taylor). The development, below the Castle keep, can be seen through the passage entrance.

Returning to Magdalen Steps, there is a view down across Elvet Bridge and Old Elvet. The crossroad at the end of the bridge was created in 1975 when the new Elvet Bridge was opened to complete the inner relief road. Hitherto, the choice was to take one of the two Elvets. To the right, much of New Elvet has been redeveloped by the University on the river side since the 1960s; its efforts have been much less sympathetic to the street scene than the extension to the Three Tuns Hotel (1979) and Orchard House (1989) opposite, where the original Georgian flavour has not been entirely lost.

Old Elvet is the most elegant street in Durham; it is also the widest – a quality connected with its former horse fairs. The street was once a major route to the South but it lost this role when the road was washed away by the river alongside Maiden Castle Wood; a branch railway line from Sunderland to the head of Old Elvet in 1897 came too late to restore any fortune. The sole reminder of the former coaching inns is the Royal County Hotel, which extends from its classical frontage on Old Elvet alongside the new bridge back to a second elevated frontage on the riverside (1989).

The original imposing façade of the Royal County was itself an amalgam of at least two houses in the second half of the 19th century. They were formerly

51 *The west front of the Cathedral and the Abbey from South Street. The river is incised 100 feet into its gorge between this viewpoint and the Peninsula.*

52 *A colourful assembly of 17th- and 18th-century properties in Saddler Street.*

72

53 *Old Elvet, which begins with the monumental, ends in domestic scale. The Grecian cast-iron balcony of No. 30 formerly provided a grandstand view of public hangings on the Court Green opposite.*

town houses associated with prominent families, most notably those of Lady Mary Ratcliffe and Eleanor Bowes. It was through the former family that Lady Mary Tudor and, later, Charles II stayed there, events recorded by plaques inside the hotel. More eye-catching, for guests amid the interior elegance, are two fine 17th-century staircases, but all can appreciate the external grandeur signalled by the giant Ionic pilasters and bold Egyptian lettering. Over the central doorway is a balustraded stone balcony, extended either side in cast iron. This is the point of salute where leading Labour politicians and trade unionists acknowledge the colliery banners and bands of the annual **Durham Miners' Gala** (**54**) as they make their noisy and colourful way to the Race Course for rallying speeches, a family picnic and all the fun of the fair. First held in 1871, this mining folk festival resembles an animated Breugel in modern dress. Long before pedestrianisation was dreamed of, the whole centre was closed to vehicular traffic for the day and shop windows on the main route were boarded up against the sheer pressure of number of bodies. Although there are now few active collieries in the county, a broadening of the trade unions represented means that the Big Meeting remains a rousing occasion.

The elegance of the north side of the street is continued first by the white classical symmetry of Nos. 53–5, where the small cannons, brought from a ship wrecked off Tynemouth, signify the local headquarters of the Territorial and Army Volunteer Reserve, and then by three-storey 18th-century brick terracing.

The south side of the street is more modest, and here the harmony was broken at the turn of the century by the Methodist Church (1903) and the remarkable Shire Hall (local architects, H. Barnes and F.E. Coates, 1898, extension 1905). The Shire Hall speaks of civic pride through its red brickwork (looking brand new), an imposing flight of steps culminating in a wrought-iron grille and the copper dome. Inside that pride is continued by highly glazed tiles on walls and ceiling, high-gloss mahogany floors and marble staircases. 'High Victorian Railway' is the most apt description of the style. The building became the Old Shire Hall in 1963, when county administrators moved out to a new centre and it became the administrative headquarters for the University. A more dramatic takeover, at least of its round council chamber, occurred in 1919 when County Durham became the first authority in England to return a Labour majority. Their first chairman was, appropriately, the miners' leader, Peter Lee.

Old Elvet Green makes a pleasant ending to the street. Facing one whole side of the Green is the Assize Courts, with the prison behind. The giant portico with Tuscan columns was largely the work of Ignatius Bonomi (completed 1821), after the dismissal of earlier architects, F. Sandys and G. Moneypenny. Bonomi was also responsible for the flanking prison-house and, opposite, for St Cuthbert's Church (1827), the first Roman Catholic church built in Durham since the Reformation. On the third side of the Green are two further points of interest. The only stone building in Old Elvet, by Thomas Ebdy, is grand in concept but modest in mass. It is the Masonic Hall, as can be guessed by the system of dating (5869) over the doorway. A few doors away, at No. 30, the cast-iron balcony would have given past dwellers not only a pleasant outlook to the Green, but also a view of public hangings outside the prison (**53**). (The last was in 1869.)

55 *The Miners's Memorial in the Cathedral. Designed by Donald McIntyre and dedicated in 1947, the skilfully carved black Spanish mahogany hearth pays tribute to those who lost their lives underground and to current workers. A book of remembrance is to the left.*

Ahead, at the end of Old Elvet, are the plain-looking Magistrates' Courts, built in 1964 on the site of the former Elvet Station. More appealing to the eye is the broad expanse of the University's playing fields, extending along the backs of the Old Elvet properties on the north side. The area is known as the Race Course from the time (1733–1887) when it was the city's horse-racing track. Pelaw Woods, on the other side of the river, may have contributed to the demise of the sport of kings here, since its rising ground provided grandstand views for spectators without the need for payment, although the University not renewing the lease of its playing fields was probably more decisive.

54 *The Durham Miners' Gala. The banner of New Herrington Miners' Lodge is carried along Old Elvet to the Race Course, having just taken its turn to pass the point of salute at the balcony of the Royal County Hotel. At the Race Course rousing speeches are delivered by political and other public figures. A service in the Cathedral follows in the afternoon.*

7 Around the Centre

Beyond the Peninsula and its immediate surroundings are a number of interesting places and buildings which, though scattered, are easily accessible on foot. This review works clockwise, beginning with the city's railway station (1857) at the head of North Road. Its size reflects the minor role which the railway played in the history of the city – and vice versa: the modestly proportioned stone building with a castellated entrance through three Tudoresque archways – now the parcels office – was the original grand entrance. The cast-iron work and platform canopies in T. Prosser's design still retain their dignity on the north platform, but the south side was refurbished in the mid-1970s with standard British Rail metalwork when the platform was set back several feet in anticipation of the speedier 125s. The station architecture was sacrificed to ease the curve of the track over the viaduct; the trains' increase in speed regrettably curtails the traveller's enjoyment of the breathtaking view of the city.

The railway viaduct is the most prominent Victorian legacy to the city and is Durham's biggest structure after the Cathedral. Built in 1857 by Robert Stevenson, the curving, multi-arched viaduct in sandstone and brick towers 100 feet above artisan housing and the North Road. The massive span reflects the difficulty the railway encountered in penetrating the city from the south. (The first line from the south was from Bishop Auckland; it was not until 1872 that a direct line from London and the south reached Durham.)

The climb up behind the railway station through Wharton Park, given to the city by W. Lloyd Wharton in the mid-19th century, is well worth the effort. The panorama from the battlements is the highlight. Many aspects of the city's geography fall into place from this vantage point, known as Ruskin's View. From the highest point there is an excellent view northwards, while over our shoulder the single, tapering column is an obelisk, erected by Wharton in 1850 and given to the University as a north meridian mark for its Observatory nearly a mile to the south. Round a little, the block-structure of the 'new' County Hall at Aykley Heads comes into view (designed by County Architects G.R. Clayton and G.W. Gelson, 1963). Nearer, but hidden in the rolling topography of the parkland, is the much smaller block-structure in white concrete and darkened glass of the **Durham Light Infantry Museum** (**58**). Designed by J.O. Tarren and P.M. Caller (1968), this delightful building nestles in landscaped grounds, with a small pond in front. Inside, the building is both a military museum, depicting the history of the county's own regiment from 1758 to 1968, and an art gallery.

Crook Hall (**57**) is a medieval manor house a mere quarter of a mile downriver from Millburngate Bridge, on rising ground in the green valley wedge. It is a composition in three parts. Of the 14th-century manor, probably built by Peter de Croke, the great hall and minstrel's gallery remain. Westwards is a 17th-century irregular gabled extension, which is attached in

56 *The grave of John Bacchus Dykes in St Oswalds' churchyard. He was precentor of the Cathedral, 1849-62, and then vicar of St Oswald's until 1874. He induced the Harrison organ factory to locate in Durham, and is best known as a prolific hymn-writer, composer of 'Lead, Kindly Light', 'Eternal Father, Strong to Save', and 'Holy, Holy, Holy'.*

turn to a tall three-storey wing in mellow brick, dated 1736. The dignified assemblage is set off by pleasant walled gardens. Among the owners have been John de Copeland, who captured King David of Scotland after the Battle of Neville's Cross in 1346, and the Billingham family, who gave the city its water supply.

On the opposite side of the river, a little further downstream, past the Sands – the freemen's common pasture and site of the traditional Holy Week Fair – is the medieval **Hospital of Kepier** (**59**). The original hospital, founded by Bishop Flambard, was on the plateau above, in Gilesgate, with St Giles' Church as its chapel. It was moved down to the riverside by Bishop le Puiset in 1180 and consisted of an infirmary, dormitory, hall and church. Its inmates, a master and 13 brethren, tended to the needs of the poor and offered hospitality to pilgrims visiting St Cuthbert's shrine. It ceased to operate at the Dissolution and a house was eventually built on the site. The large 14th-century gatehouse survives as the farm entrance, but otherwise only fragments of the Hospital remain among the farm buildings in their peaceful setting.

The **Church of St Giles** (**60**) is to the south of the village green, affording fine glimpses of the Cathedral from the elevated churchyard. The north door and the north wall of the nave, pierced by three small windows, date from the time when it was a chapel to the Hospital. The chancel is late 12th century, otherwise the church is largely 13th to 15th century. In the sanctuary is a wooden effigy of John Heath, who acquired Kepier Hospital after the Dissolution.

57 *Crook Hall, occupied since at least the beginning of the 13th century, when it was part of the manor of Sidegate. Shown here are the 17th-century two-storey extension built by the Mickleton family and the 18th-century three-storey wing added by the Hopper family.*

58 The Durham Light Infantry Museum and Arts Centre, set within the parkland of Aykley Heads Estate.

The settlement of Gilesgate, a 'planned suburb' of the city following the Norman clearance of the earliest peninsular dwellings, is one of the county's 'green villages'. Aligned characteristically west–east, with houses facing the green, the enclosed area was used as an animal compound with common grazing, and for community occasions. The present road, which bisects the green, was the main route to Sunderland until the 1960s, when the A690 dual-carriageway was opened along the line of the city's first railway. The rail terminus, just above the present roundabout, is now a D.I.Y. store. The exterior of G.T. Andrew's Gilesgate Station (1844) retains its classical stone dignity; inside, the cast-iron work of the canopy can be detected, even though the platforms have been levelled.

On the steep southern slope from the Gilesgate plateau towards the river are set the prominent buildings originally founded as diocesan teacher-training colleges, neo-Tudor St Bede (1847) and Gothic St Hild (1858). The former was originally for male teachers, the latter for women, one of the first such institutions in the country. They amalgamated in 1976 and united with the University three years later. The gradient gives the students spectacular views from their college rooms and gardens towards the Peninsula.

Below Pelaw Woods the riverside path leads upstream to the former manor and present farm of Old Durham, in whose grounds the remains of the bathhouse of a Roman villa were discovered in 1940. They have since been lost in the working of sand. The 17th-century manor has also disappeared, but the walk is rewarded by another fine and again different view of the Cathedral, seen here from the east, a massive compact structure rising out of the woods of Maidencastle in the middle ground. Also of interest is the remaining outline of the walled gardens of the former mansion. The local authority has restored the gazebo and plans are in hand to regenerate both the formal design of the upper garden and the stepped lower garden. A former jetty for small boats on a re-excavated Old Durham Back is also possible.

St Oswald's Church (**61**) in Church Street is probably the oldest

ecclesiastical site in Durham. The *Anglo-Saxon Chronicle* records the consecration at Elvet of Peohtwine as Bishop of Whithorn in 763. Nothing of that
antiquity remains, but the designation of the church to a 7th-century
Northumbrian king and the discovery of pre-Conquest sculpture in the
building suggest its early foundation. Of the present building, the four eastern
bays of the long nave and the chancel arch are dated 12th-century. Much of
the remainder is 15th-century Perpendicular, although mining subsidence
and decay prompted extensive restoration by Bonomi in 1834. In 1864 the
east end was rebuilt and the statues of King Oswald and St Cuthbert were
mounted outside. The latter is shown holding the head of Oswald who died
fighting the pagan king of Mercia in 642. (The actual skull was placed in
Cuthbert's tomb. It was Oswald who had invited Aidan from Iona to
Lindisfarne to found the Community which became the Christian power-
house of northern England.) Also in 1864 a west window by Ford Madox
Brown was inserted. The vicar at this time was John Bacchus Dykes, the
prolific Victorian hymn writer. More than 50 of his compositions were

60 *St Giles' north porch,
bearing a statue of the
saint with the hart which,
according to legend, he
saved from its hunters.
The flanking coats of
arms are those of the see
of Durham (right), and
of the fifth Marquess of
Londonderry, with the
added escutcheon of his
wife (left).*

59 *The Medieval
gatehouse of Kepier
Hospital.*

included in *Hymns Ancient and Modern*, of which the best known is perhaps the tune 'Hollingside' to 'Jesu, lover of my soul'. The name comes from his vicarage in Hollingside Lane; many of his tunes are named after local scenes. His grave is in the churchyard extension diagonally opposite the church, his stone and the surround being the only one not subsequently removed to the perimeter wall (**56**).

At the southern end of Church Street the extensive University grounds begin. The Science Site is heralded by the bold new University Library (H. Faulkner-Brown, 1983) and classical West Building (J.S. Allen, 1952), which complement each other in massing, texture and colour across the landscaped corner. There is now nothing to suggest that until the early years of the 20th century Elvet Colliery occupied this corner, or that the terraces opposite and at the head of Church Street were built for the mineworkers. Inside the gates of the Science Site the standard of architecture is variable: the most solid building is the earliest, the Dawson Building (1924); the best is one of the most recent, the Palladian Psychology Building (William Whitfield, 1970).

Southwards, on both sides of South Road, residential colleges are dotted among the gently sloping parkland. They reflect the post-war expansion of the University, which has grown from 650 students in 1945 to nearly 1,600 in 1963 (when King's College, Newcastle, became an entirely separate institution), to over 5,000 in 1990. The building response has been within the context of the University's own development plans – in 1947 by J.S. Allen and in 1969 when the consultant was William Whitfield. The potential of each site has been realised by the appointment of a different architect for each college.

61 *St Oswald's Church from the south. It was Oswald who invited St Aidan to found a missionary base on Lindisfarne for the conversion of the kingdom of Northumbria, and the area with the earliest record of Christian activity in the city is dedicated to this 7th-century king and martyr.*

The earliest and boldest is St Mary's College (V. Harris, 1952). Standing clear on the lowest slopes of the park landscape, it has the fullest view of the Cathedral, at the same time giving the impression of wanting to offer the Cathedral the clearest view of itself. With a large hipped roof, tall chimneys, a ponderous stone face and entry up wide steps from a vast forecourt, it sets out to impress. The panache – and perhaps the money – had disappeared ten years later when a second, lower block was added (M. Sisson, 1962). Most recently, the original building has been flanked by residential blocks for the University of Teikyo, Japan, under a unique agreement between the two universities. The basic design (J. Williams, 1990), though no longer monumental in conception, complements the original building in its brick and also in its high-pitched roof, the latter functionally induced by the need for large tanks to meet the high water requirements of the oriental occupants.

Grey College (T. Worthington, 1961), the second post-war college to be constructed, provides a contrast in its domestic or municipal Georgian style and in being broken into separate three-storey blocks. **St Aidan's College (63)** (Sir Basil Spence, 1965) differs again. Although set on a hill, with its own distinctive views of the Cathedral, the college itself is curiously unobtrusive as a skyline feature. At closer quarters it is attractive in its own right, with a monumental concrete and brick north-facing dining-room and staggered fenestration of the west residential wing echoing elements the architect had used earlier in Coventry Cathedral. The chapel he designed for the college was never built, leaving the semi-formal gardens, designed by Brian Hackett, to be half embraced by two residential wings.

62 *A Japanese temple lantern at Elvet Hill ornaments the garden of the Gulbenkian Museum of Oriental Art.*

Van Mildert College (64) (P. Middleton, 1966) and Trevelyan College (H. Stillman and J. Eastwick Field, 1967) are close to each other in location and age but are markedly different in design. The former, with no view of the Cathedral, is focused instead around a small lake. The topography means that the main entrance is to a single-storey building, but immediately inside the space falls away to the light-filled dining-room below, looking out onto the lake. The external view towards the college from across the lake is the popular picture-postcard view. Van Mildert College received a Civic Trust Commendation; Trevelyan College achieved a Trust Award for its dark-brick essay in interlocking hexagonal blocks and spaces. It is intriguing to view but puzzling to navigate, and must have been awkward to furnish.

With Collingwood College (Sir Richard Sheppard, 1973) the brickwork returned to a more conventional design, the interlocking blocks forming a single composition with mature woodland; it is almost as if what we call landscaping for the newly built form was conceived and planted half a century before. The effect inside is of bringing nature indoors. The autumn colouring, seen through the strong wooden mullions of the dining and common rooms, is especially striking.

Three other features in the extensive parkland of the University are noteworthy. One is the Botanical Gardens in Hollingside Lane, where different parts of the grounds are devoted to the cultivation of trees and plants from particular foreign habitats. A special collection is the sub-Alpine flora rescued from upper Teesdale ahead of the construction of Cow Green Reservoir. The second feature is the Museum of Oriental Art or Gulbenkian Museum (M. Fletcher, 1961), the only museum in the country entirely devoted to Eastern art and archaeology (62). It is largely concealed among a mature stand of trees which surround it and the adjacent Elvet Hill House, a

63 *St Aidan's College, looking toward the dining hall from the landscaped gardens.*

64 *Van Mildert College, looking across the lake to the dining hall (right) and residential wings.*

19th-century stone-clad house built by Bonomi as his residence, but now the home of the University's School of Oriental Studies.

The third feature is the University's Observatory, a classical stone building erected to a design by Salvin in 1841. Astronomical observations were begun the following year under the initiative of a remarkable character in the young University, the Rev. Professor Temple Chevallier, who lectured in astronomy, physics, mathematics, Hebrew and classics, besides being Vicar of Esh. The Observatory has the second longest set of weather recordings in Britain; however, since the recording environment of the leading observatory (Oxford) has been affected by building encroachment, Durham's recordings could claim first rather than second place on grounds of consistency.

After Observatory Field with its memorable view of the Cathedral, leafy Quarry Heads Lane below is bordered by the grounds of Durham School, transferred here from Palace Green in the 1840s. The nucleus is a combination of Salvin's neo-Gothic (1844) and Blomfield's neo-Tudor (1870–80). The school chapel, designed by W. Brierley (1926) as a First World War memorial, is set theatrically at the top of a tiered grassy bank.

After the right-angled bends of the road around Durham School, Margery Lane suddenly opens up to reveal the west end of the Cathedral towering above the silhouette of South Street roofs and trees, with an expanse of allotment gardens in the sunken foreground. This surprising scene is Durham's equivalent of Constable's depiction of Salisbury Cathedral from the water meadows. The workaday environment here, however, is also of historic interest, for the stone for the construction of the Cathedral came from this site. The walls of the former quarry – which led from Quarry Heads Lane – are marked by the steep rise along the southern boundary. The lowest part of the area was subsequently used as the Abbey fishpond. The allotments were laid out in the mid-19th century, when this was glebe land of St Margaret's Church.

The two final items in this clockwise itinerary, though prominent, can be

easily missed. One is Flass Vale, entered from Waddington Street. Although a public open space, this is not the usual municipal park with neat lawns and seats – quite the reverse: it is a wilderness park, with the minimum of opening up, where the wildlife of badger and fox are as much at home as the domestic pet. The other is the Miners' Hall in Redhills Lane, hidden behind the main-line viaduct and embankment. When completed by H.T. Graydon in 1915, this headquarters of the Durham Miners' Association (**65**) rivalled the recently completed Shire Hall in size. From the dome over the porch to the dome on the roof, the building exudes the confidence of a union then 150,000-strong. Today, there are a mere 6,000 miners in the county. The four sculptures of miners' leaders standing uneasily in the forecourt approach, having been brought from the original 1874 headquarters in the North Road, must surely be wondering whether the time for another move is approaching.

65 *Durham Miners' Association headquarters in Redhills Lane, a little-visited part of the city; even the rail traveller, who could gain the best view of the imposing classical façade, is almost certainly looking out of the opposite window toward the Cathedral and Castle.*

66 *The woodland of the River Banks in its springtime freshness, as seen from Quarry Heads Lane, which runs around the southern lip of the gorge.*

8 Around the District

Around the ancient city, but within the City of Durham District, are several sites which have links with the city's past evolution and which today reward the attention of any visitor. The various locations are again described in clockwise order.

Finchale Abbey or Priory, 4 miles north of the city, though more modest than the great Yorkshire abbeys, clearly demonstrates the Benedictine eye for a choice site. The ruins (**68**) stand in open countryside on gentle grassy folds of the west bank of the River Wear, here gliding over horizontal bands of sandstone. On the opposite bank rises a steeply wooded backcloth. It was the very seclusion of the area that determined its choice when Godric, a sea-captain turned hermit, was granted permission in 1110 by Bishop Flambard to establish a cell here. According to legend, St Godric's piety extended to immersing himself up to his chin in the river for night-long prayer. Today, in June every year, the congregation from the city church of St Oswald hold a – more sedate – service here by the riverside.

When Godric died in 1170, at the age of 106, the cell was taken over by Durham Priory. Within 50 years the buildings – church, cloister with chapter house and refectory, and prior's house with prior's chapel – had assumed their present extent, and the establishment consisted of a prior and four monks, with another four monks from the Abbey in Durham lodging temporarily to experience a 'holiday in the country'. It all ended at the Reformation. The ruins, with many walls still standing to their original height, give the feel of the former monastic settlement.

Four miles to the north-east lies the shrunken medieval village of Pittington Hallgarth (or simply Hallgarth), which is historically and physically separated from the present village of Pittington. Here, earthworks amid the trees and open countryside mark the site of the medieval hamlet and of the manor house, a summer residence of the Prior of Durham. Only the Church of St Laurence remains, but that alone warrants a visit. The Saxon origin of the building is indicated by the small light windows and the sundial on the south wall, but the Norman interior is its glory.

Particularly noteworthy is the north arcade, which was created to enlarge the original aisleless Saxon nave. Its bold chevroned arches loop between pillars which are alternately octagonal and circular, the latter being embellished with elaborate spiral moulding. Above, at the western end, are wall paintings showing the consecration of St Cuthbert by Archbishop Theodore and his vision at the table of Abbess Aelflede in Whitby Abbey. Both arcade and painting date from the late 12th century and are associated with Bishop le Puiset. One of the Bishop's master masons, named Christian, is buried beneath a large tombstone of Frosterley marble in the south aisle. He could well have been the mason responsible not only for the work here but also for the contemporary and similar bold carving in the Galilee Chapel of the Cathedral.

67 *The monogram of Christ and the crossed keys of St Peter on the colourful chancel ceiling of St Peter's, Monkwearmouth (Sunderland). The church is on the site of the monastery founded by Benedict Biscop in 674.*

The south arcade of the church followed a few years later, in the early 13th century, but sufficient time had elapsed for styles to have changed, so the pillars on this side are joined by Early English pointed arches. The church is completed by a late Norman chancel and a tower which is essentially Norman, with an Early English upper stage. The Norman font, a plain functional bowl, has an unusual history, having served as a cattle trough on a nearby farm for most of the 19th century before being recovered in 1885.

Bishop le Puiset's influence is also seen nearby at Sherburn Hospital, which today consists of a small nucleus in a thickly wooded setting 3 miles east of the city on the A181. Le Puiset founded the hospital for lepers, but with the gradual disappearance of leprosy, Bishop Langley converted it into alms-houses. The Norman origins are today visible only in the chapel, Scottish raids and fire having necessitated rebuilding, but the whole still presents a pleasant unity. Beyond a 13th-century battlemented gateway entrance are the mid-18th-century almshouses, master's house, chapel and Victorian Gothic hospital block for retired clergy, arranged around a large green quadrangle.

The return from Sherburn Hospital to Durham could well be via the B1198 and the village of Shincliffe, which lies barely 2 miles south of the beckoning Cathedral. It is a good example of a Durham 'green village', the green here having high verges either side of the tree-lined High Street which provides an

68 *The broken silhouette of Finchale Priory ruins under a threatening western sky.*

additional attraction to the flanking variety of 18th- and 19th-century cottages. The village also contains some interesting examples of modern residential 'infill'. The most successful of these is the earliest, the 1962 scheme of the Dean and Chapter, where houses are arranged around their own green to frame the spire of the village church. A third element of interest, which needs the eye of knowledge to be detected, is the incorporation of the former Shincliffe railway station (opened in 1839), in a modern housing scheme on Low Road (hence the name of the nearby Railway Tavern).

All visitors to Durham should include Brancepeth (**69**) on their itinerary. Little more than 4 miles south-west of the city on the A690, a sudden crossroads announces a small village that could easily be missed. To turn left is to enter another world. A wide straight street, lined on one side by modest 19th-century estate cottages and on the other by mature trees and greenery, leads to the imposing pillars of park gates propped permanently open. In the park beyond, the road gently curves to give the visitor a wide view on the approach to a forbidding-looking castle with an overpowering gatehouse. At close quarters a cursory glance confirms that its surface antiquity is recent, the result of rebuilding and enlargement in the 1820s by John Paterson. The surviving parts of an earlier castle are confined to some basements and bastions. This earlier castle, itself a rebuilding, was erected by Ralph Neville, 1st Earl of Westmorland and Marshall of England from 1399 until his death in 1426. The Nevilles were one of the leading families in the country, and for nearly four centuries Brancepeth Castle was the family stronghold, being preferred to a second castle at Raby, presumably because of its closer proximity to the city.

After Brancepeth Castle was forfeited to the Crown in 1529 as a result of the Neville family having supported the Rising of the North, the building passed

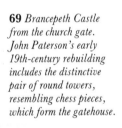

69 *Brancepeth Castle from the church gate. John Paterson's early 19th-century rebuilding includes the distinctive pair of round towers, resembling chess pieces, which form the gatehouse.*

through several hands before its purchase in 1796 by William Russell, a Sunderland banker and coal-owner. It was his son Matthew who instigated the rebuilding on a grand scale. A baron's hall, armour gallery, private chapel, library and other rooms were all provided on an uncomfortably large scale on two sides of a spacious quadrangle. The furnishing was assisted by the Tennyson family, into which Matthew Russell married. In the 20th century the castle again changed hands, serving as the headquarters of the Durham Light Infantry and then as a research laboratory for a Sunderland glass-making firm before becoming once again a family home. The present owner is slowly and sensitively restoring the rooms after several generations of neglect.

Further into the parkland, a little beyond the Castle and shielded by its own thick cluster of trees, is the Church of St Brandon. Here, the early work of the Neville family has not been obliterated, although the building was embellished in a remarkable manner by a 17th-century restorer. The result is surely one of the most interesting churches in the whole country.

The structure of the church dates largely from the 13th to 15th centuries. Inside, the tall nave has octagonal piers with Early English arches and a Perpendicular clerestory. On either side of the chancel are prominent recumbent figures of the former lords of the manor and benefactors – the big stone effigy is that of Robert Neville, 'The Peacock of the North', who died in 1318; opposite, in oak, are Ralph Neville, the 2nd Earl of Westmorland (died 1489) and his wife. The monuments are completed with the large altar tomb of Ralph, the third Earl (died 1523).

It is the extent and sumptuousness of the woodwork which give individuality and unity to the building, and this is due to John Cosin, who

70 *The castellated roofline of Raby Castle, a second home for the powerful Neville family in the late Middle Ages and now the residence of the Lord Barnard. In the distance rise the Pennine moorlands of Teesdale.*

71 *Auckland Castle seen from its ornamental garden. The castle at Bishop Auckland became the bishop's permanent residence when Durham Castle was presented to the University in 1837.*

was Rector of Brancepeth (1626–40) before he became Bishop of Durham. His distinctive woodwork, or wood sculpture, will be immediately recognised from its counterparts in Durham Cathedral and Castle. Here, Cosin's imprint is visible first in the Jacobean-style stone porch which he added to the north side of the church, but it is inside that his influence is unmistakable – from the font cover, the set of panelled box-pews and benches, and the double-decker pulpit with sounding board, to the chancel screen with canopied entrance, the choir stalls and the altar table. The wooden rib-vaulting of the chancel, decorated over the altar, completes this remarkable ensemble.

A final excursion might take in the ruins of Beaurepaire, the 'beautiful retreat' or former summer lodging of the priors of Durham, 2 miles west of the city. It is best approached along the walkway of the former railway, leaving the B6302 road at its former crossing just before it reaches the present village of Bearpark (a corruption of the original place-name). The walk may provoke reflections on the feverish century of industrial activity recently passed on the upper or left-hand side of the former railway – where there were a colliery, cokeworks and brickworks, together employing a thousand men, plus an accompanying colliery or pit village – all created since 1872 and now all disappeared. (The present village in the middle distance has emerged since the 1930s.)

Beaurepaire lies to the right, just across the River Browney on a slight eminence near to Stotgate Farm. The settlement, consisting of prior's lodging or manor house, chapel and dormitory, was in the middle of a 1,300-acre estate notable for its deer and timber. (Its 40-foot oaks roofed the monks' dormitory in the Abbey at Durham.) English kings were entertained here; and in 1346 the Scottish King David Bruce, accompanied by his army, was an uninvited guest on the eve of the Battle of Neville's Cross. In the absence of

Edward III, who was abroad, the English forces were led by Ralph Lord Neville, his son John and Lord Percy. (Their victory in the battle is commemorated by the stump of a 10-foot shaft on a stepped platform located on the city side of the traffic lights in the western suburb now known as Neville's Cross.)

The damage inflicted on Beaurepaire by the Scottish troops before the battle was soon made good by Prior Fosser, who also considerably enlarged the manor house. Two centuries later, however, during the Civil War period, the buildings were again sacked by Scottish armies and left unrepaired at the Restoration. Old prints show that the roofless buildings survived until the late 18th century. Recent archaeological excavations and restoration help today's visitor to appreciate their former glory.

72 The Church of St John the Evangelist, Escomb, near Bishop Auckland, one of only three complete Saxon churches surviving in the country.